RSpec Essentials

Develop testable, modular, and maintainable
Ruby software for the real world using RSpec

Mani Tadayon

BIRMINGHAM - MUMBAI

RSpec Essentials

First published: April 2016

Production reference: 1130416

Published by Packt Publishing Ltd.
Livery Place
35 Livery Street
Birmingham B3 2PB, UK.

ISBN 978-1-78439-590-2

www.packtpub.com

Credits

Author
Mani Tadayon

Reviewers
Stefan Daschek
Nola Stowe

Commissioning Editor
Amarabha Banerjee

Acquisition Editor
Reshma Raman

Content Development Editor
Rashmi Suvarna

Technical Editor
Anushree Arun Tendulkar

Copy Editor
Safis Editing

Project Coordinator
Judie Jose

Proofreader
Safis Editing

Indexer
Rekha Nair

Graphics
Abhinash Sahu

Production Coordinator
Manu Joseph

Cover Work
Manu Joseph

About the Author

Mani Tadayon first learned to program as a shy 7th grader on an Apple IIe using BASIC. He went on to learn Pascal, C++, Java, JavaScript, Visual Basic, and PHP before becoming a Ruby developer in 2008. With 15 years of experience in the software industry, he has developed expertise in web development, infrastructure, and testing. Mani's interests and education are broad, with degrees in foreign languages, computer science, and geography. He lives just far enough from Silicon Valley with his family and their many, many Shiba Inus.

About the Reviewers

Stefan Daschek started hacking on computers back in the days of the Commodore 64/128. Since then, he has studied computer sciences at TU Vienna and founded his own company, Büro DIE ANTWORT. Currently, he is mainly developing and maintaining complex web applications written in Ruby on Rails, and sometimes soldering stuff and building small robots. His original Commodore 128 is still working and used for a collective session of Summer Games every so often.

Nola Stowe has been programming with Ruby since Rails 0.8 and testing with RSpec since its early days. She is an independent consultant, helping to augment teams of Ruby and Clojure developers. She has also been a technical reviewer for *Instant RSpec Test-Driven Development*, *Packt Publishing* and *The Rails Way, First Edition*. Nola blogs at `http://blog.rubygeek.com` and `http://www.clojuregeek.com`.

> Thanks to my husband Nick for doing the mundane things in life to allow me time do what I love doing. You are the greatest!

www.PacktPub.com

eBooks, discount offers, and more

Did you know that Packt offers eBook versions of every book published, with PDF and ePub files available? You can upgrade to the eBook version at www.PacktPub.com and as a print book customer, you are entitled to a discount on the eBook copy. Get in touch with us at customercare@packtpub.com for more details.

At www.PacktPub.com, you can also read a collection of free technical articles, sign up for a range of free newsletters and receive exclusive discounts and offers on Packt books and eBooks.

https://www2.packtpub.com/books/subscription/packtlib

Do you need instant solutions to your IT questions? PacktLib is Packt's online digital book library. Here, you can search, access, and read Packt's entire library of books.

Why subscribe?

- Fully searchable across every book published by Packt
- Copy and paste, print, and bookmark content
- On demand and accessible via a web browser

Table of Contents

Preface

RSpec is one of the reasons why the Ruby programming language has become so popular. There is a strong emphasis on testing, documentation, and iterative development in the Ruby community. With RSpec, it is easy to create excellent tests that specify behavior and improve the development process.

In this book, we'll learn how to use RSpec in a real-world setting. We'll also learn about the concept of testability, which relates to our application code as well as to our tests. Throughout, we'll focus on writing tests that are valuable and stay away from testing for its own sake.

RSpec offers a variety of tools for creating test scenarios, assertions, and error messages. We can create the tests we need and get the exact output we want using RSpec without having to do too much work. RSpec has been under development for almost 10 years, so it has evolved significantly. Many ways of writing tests have developed due to the flexibility of RSpec and the underlying Ruby language. Some of these are clever but some others are too clever. We'll learn about a solid subset of RSpec's features that are reliable and avoid some of the trickier features.

Today, professional software development must include automated testing. However, testing presents many challenges in the real world. There is a danger of learning about testing tools without knowing how to use them effectively. In this book, we will always keep an eye on the real world, even in our simple examples. We'll cover a range of application types, from libraries to rich web UIs, and a range of approaches to testing, from unit tests to behavior-driven development. Along the way, we'll discuss potential pitfalls and develop production-grade solutions to avoid them.

As you progress through this book, you will learn about many RSpec features, my recommended approach to using them, and their relation to testability. I hope that you can use this book both as a handbook for simple tasks and as a guide to developing a sophisticated understanding of automated software testing.

What this book covers

Chapter 1, Exploring Testability from Unit Tests to Behavior-Driven Development, defines the basic concepts of unit, test, and testability, and puts them in context.

Chapter 2, Specifying Behavior with Examples and Matchers, shows how RSpec's basic features implement units and assertions.

Chapter 3, Taking Control of State with Doubles and Hooks, discusses how RSpec implements mocks and hooks to allow us to set up a test scenario.

Chapter 4, Setting Up and Cleaning Up, delves further into how we can simulate external resources such as databases and web servers while keeping our test environment clean using RSpec support code.

Chapter 5, Simulating External Services, extends our discussion of handling external web services by using the VCR gem.

Chapter 6, Driving a Web Browser with Capybara, introduces the Capybara library, and shows how to use it to test rich web UIs.

Chapter 7, Building an App from the Outside In with Behavior-Driven Development, explains BDD and how RSpec can be used to define high-level features.

Chapter 8, Tackling the Challenges of End-to-end Testing, continues with the development of the app built in the previous chapter, focusing on common testing pain points, such as authentication.

Chapter 9, Configurability, introduces a concept that is related to testability and an implementation of a real-world configuration system.

Chapter 10, Odds and Ends, wraps up the book by covering a few advanced topics that didn't quite fit into the previous chapters, but which were too important to leave out.

What you need for this book

You'll need two basic pieces of software for this book: Ruby and RSpec.

You can install the Ruby programming language from its web site:

```
https://www.ruby-lang.org/en/downloads/
```

The latest version at the time of writing is 2.3.0. Any version of Ruby greater than 2.0 should be fine.

I recommend that you use rbenv to install Ruby. This tool will make it easier to keep a clean Ruby environment. Professional Ruby developers rely on rbenv or similar tools to install and manage Ruby on their systems. You can find more info on rbenv on its GitHub page:

```
https://github.com/rbenv/rbenv
```

You can install RSpec using the rubygems installer (`gem install rspec`). The latest version of RSpec at the time of writing is 3.4.0, but any version greater than 3.0 should work fine. More details on RSpec can be found on its GitHub repo:

```
https://github.com/rspec/rspec
```

Who this book is for

This book is for the programmer who has some experience with Ruby. If you have written some small programs and are familiar with defining basic functions, modules, and classes, then you should be fine. If you have no background in Ruby, you will still be able to follow along, but will need to do a little extra work to follow the more complicated sections. I've done my best to build up complex examples step by step and clearly explain every aspect of the code samples with comments.

Conventions

In this book, you will find a number of text styles that distinguish between different kinds of information. Here are some examples of these styles and an explanation of their meaning.

Code words in text, database table names, folder names, filenames, file extensions, pathnames, dummy URLs, user input, and Twitter handles are shown as follows: "We can include other contexts through the use of the `include` directive."

A block of code is set as follows:

```
require 'rspec'

describe 'new RSpec syntax' do
  it "uses the new assertion syntax" do
    # new                          # deprecated
    expect(1 + 1).to eq(2)         # (1 + 1).should == 2
  end
```

Any command-line input or output is written as follows:

```
# comments to clarify the command
$ echo 'Hello'
# => Hello
```

Often, command-line output will be displayed in screenshots to show output more clearly and to discourage cut-and-paste without thinking through the commands. The screenshots will like look the following:

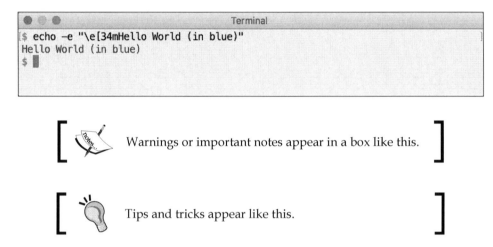

[<image>notes</image>   Warnings or important notes appear in a box like this.]

[<image>tip</image>   Tips and tricks appear like this.]

Reader feedback

Feedback from our readers is always welcome. Let us know what you think about this book—what you liked or disliked. Reader feedback is important for us as it helps us develop titles that you will really get the most out of.

To send us general feedback, simply e-mail feedback@packtpub.com, and mention the book's title in the subject of your message.

If there is a topic that you have expertise in and you are interested in either writing or contributing to a book, see our author guide at www.packtpub.com/authors.

Customer support

Now that you are the proud owner of a Packt book, we have a number of things to help you to get the most from your purchase.

Downloading the example code

You can download the example code files for this book from your account at `http://www.packtpub.com`. If you purchased this book elsewhere, you can visit `http://www.packtpub.com/support` and register to have the files e-mailed directly to you.

You can download the code files by following these steps:

1. Log in or register to our website using your e-mail address and password.
2. Hover the mouse pointer on the **SUPPORT** tab at the top.
3. Click on **Code Downloads & Errata**.
4. Enter the name of the book in the **Search** box.
5. Select the book for which you're looking to download the code files.
6. Choose from the drop-down menu where you purchased this book from.
7. Click on **Code Download**.

You can also download the code files by clicking on the **Code Files** button on the book's webpage at the Packt Publishing website. This page can be accessed by entering the book's name in the `Search` box. Please note that you need to be logged in to your Packt account.

Once the file is downloaded, please make sure that you unzip or extract the folder using the latest version of:

- WinRAR / 7-Zip for Windows
- Zipeg / iZip / UnRarX for Mac
- 7-Zip / PeaZip for Linux

Downloading the color images of this book

We also provide you with a PDF file that has color images of the screenshots/ diagrams used in this book. The color images will help you better understand the changes in the output. You can download this file from `http://www.packtpub.com/sites/default/files/downloads/RSpecEssentials_ColoredImages.pdf`.

Errata

Although we have taken every care to ensure the accuracy of our content, mistakes do happen. If you find a mistake in one of our books—maybe a mistake in the text or the code—we would be grateful if you could report this to us. By doing so, you can save other readers from frustration and help us improve subsequent versions of this book. If you find any errata, please report them by visiting http://www.packtpub.com/submit-errata, selecting your book, clicking on the **Errata Submission Form** link, and entering the details of your errata. Once your errata are verified, your submission will be accepted and the errata will be uploaded to our website or added to any list of existing errata under the Errata section of that title.

To view the previously submitted errata, go to https://www.packtpub.com/books/content/support and enter the name of the book in the search field. The required information will appear under the **Errata** section.

Piracy

Piracy of copyrighted material on the Internet is an ongoing problem across all media. At Packt, we take the protection of our copyright and licenses very seriously. If you come across any illegal copies of our works in any form on the Internet, please provide us with the location address or website name immediately so that we can pursue a remedy.

Please contact us at copyright@packtpub.com with a link to the suspected pirated material.

We appreciate your help in protecting our authors and our ability to bring you valuable content.

Questions

If you have a problem with any aspect of this book, you can contact us at questions@packtpub.com, and we will do our best to address the problem.

1
Exploring Testability from Unit Tests to Behavior-Driven Development

In this book, we are going to learn about **RSpec** in depth. But first, we need to lay some foundations. This chapter will introduce some important information that will prepare us for our exploration of RSpec.

First, we'll discuss the exciting promise of automated tests. We'll also discuss some of the pitfalls and challenges that are common when writing tests for real-world apps.

Next, we'll introduce the concept of testability, which will stay with us throughout this book. We'll then go over the technical assumptions made in the book.

We'll then start writing some simple unit tests with RSpec and explore the basic concepts of *unit* and *test*. We'll also start thinking about the usefulness of our tests and compare the cost of testing with its benefits.

Finally, we'll learn about two popular software methodologies: **test-driven development** (TDD) and **behavior-driven development** (BDD).

The promise of testing

When I first learned about automated tests for software, it felt as if a door to a new world had opened up. Automated tests offered the promise of scientific precision and engineering rigor in software development, a process which I thought was limited by its nature to guesswork and trial and error.

This initial euphoria lasted less than a year. The practical experience of creating and maintaining tests for real-world applications gave me many reasons to doubt the promise of automated tests. Tests took a lot of effort to write and update. They often failed even though the code worked. Or the tests passed even when the code did not work. In either scenario, much effort was devoted to testing, without much benefit.

As the number of tests grew, they took longer and longer to run. To make them run faster, more effort had to be devoted to optimizing their performance or developing fancy ways of running them (on multiple cores or in the cloud, for example).

But even with many, many tests and more lines of test code than actual application code, many important features had no tests. This was rarely due to negligence but due to the difficulty of testing many aspects of real-world software.

Finally, bugs still popped up and tests were often written as part of the bug fix to ensure these bugs would not happen again. Just as generals always prepare for the last war, tests were ensuring the last bug didn't happen without helping prevent the next bug.

After several years of facing these challenges, and addressing them with various strategies, I realized that, for most developers, automated tests had become a dogma, and tests were primarily written for their own sake.

To benefit from automated tests, I believe one must consider the cost of testing. In other words, the effort of writing the test must be worth the benefits it offers. What I have learned is that the benefit of tests is rarely to directly prevent bugs, but rather to contribute to improved code quality and organization, which, in turn, will lead to more reliable software. Put another way, although automated tests are closely tied to quality assurance, their focus should be on quality, not assurance. This is just common sense if you think about it. How can we give assurance with automated (or manual) tests that a real-world piece of software, composed of thousands of lines of code, will not have bugs? How can we predict every possible use case, and how every line of code will behave?

Another issue is how to write tests. A number of challenges arise when testing complex applications in the real world. Should you use fixtures or mocks to test models? How should you deal with rack middleware in controller tests? How should you test code that interacts with external APIs and services? This book offers the essentials required to solve problems like these with RSpec, the popular **Ruby** testing library.

The goal of this book is to help you effectively leverage RSpec's many features to test and improve your code. Although we will limit ourselves to the most pertinent options, I encourage you to consult the official RSpec documentation (`http://rspec.info/documentation/`) to learn more about all the possible options. You should find it easy to build upon the examples here to develop a custom solution that exactly meets your own needs and preferences.

Testability

A fundamental concept that unites the chapters of this book is testability. When code is testable, we have confidence in its architecture and implementation. We can test it thoroughly with ease. Bugs are quickly detected and easily fixed. The first step to improving testability in an application is to establish a natural feedback loop between application code and test code, using signals from testing to improve application code. The energy devoted to writing complex tests for untestable code should be channeled into making the code more testable, allowing simpler tests to be written. With this feedback loop and focus on testability, tests contribute to code quality and application reliability.

Testability is not a binary quality. When looking at a given software system, we should ask, "How testable is this?", rather than trying to categorize it as testable or not testable. This requires judgment and common sense. As our features and priorities evolve, so must our criteria for testability. For example, let's consider a new web application with a small number of users, which has all kinds of automated tests for important features but none for testing performance under high load. This system can be considered to have high testability as long as we have few users and performance is not yet a concern. Once the web application becomes very popular and we need to serve millions of requests a day, we would have to change our judgment to say that the system now has very low testability. What use are all the tests that aren't related to performance if none of our users can reach our website because we cannot serve requests fast enough?

Testability should be achieved with efficiency. We need to figure out which features to test and not spend too much effort on tests that don't offer much value. As with testability, efficiency is not static and we must adjust the criteria for it as software evolves.

We can define testability as the degree to which a system can be verified to work as expected. At the smallest level, closest to the individual lines of code that make up our software, we are concerned with whether functions return the values we expect. At higher levels of abstraction, we are concerned with behaviors such as error handling, performance, and the correctness of entire end-to-end features. Let's keep in mind that testability includes manual tests as well. Manual testing is a normal part of development and quality assurance. If an aspect of a software system cannot be tested manually, it is very likely that it will be quite difficult to test it using automated tools as well.

Often, developers struggle to automate manual tests for a system with low testability. This common pitfall leads to high-cost, low-value tests and a system whose architecture and organization is not improved by the testing efforts. Our focus in this book will be on improving testability using automated tests written with RSpec. We will make both manual and automated tests better, with less effort required to create and maintain our tests. Both the architecture and organization of our system will benefit. By diverting some of our testing energy to improving the testability of the code, we will be engaged in a positive feedback loop, whereby our effort devoted to testing provides a meaningful benefit without excessive cost.

Technical assumptions

This book assumes that the reader is comfortable reading and writing Ruby code. Familiarity with RSpec is strongly recommended, though a total beginner to RSpec should find it possible to understand most of the recipes with the help of the online RSpec documentation. Each code example has been tested and works. I have used the latest stable versions available at the time of writing: Ruby 2.3.0 with RSpec 3.4.0.

RSpec 3 uses a different syntax from RSpec 2. Version 2.13 introduced a new syntax for assertions while 2.14 introduced a new syntax for doubles and expectations. RSpec 3.0 introduced a number of new features and changes as well. I have used the new syntax and features throughout the book:

```
require 'rspec'

describe 'new RSpec syntax' do
  it "uses the new assertion syntax" do
    # new                          # deprecated
    expect(1 + 1).to eq(2)         # (1 + 1).should == 2
  end

  context "mocks and expectations" do
    let(:obj) do
```

```
      # new                         # deprecated
      double('foo')                 # obj = mock('foo')
    end

    it "uses the new allow syntax for mocks" do
      # new                         # deprecated
      allow(obj).to receive(:bar)   # obj.stub(:bar)
    end

    it "uses the new expect syntax for expectations" do
      # new                         # deprecated
      expect(obj).to receive(:baz)  # obj.should_receive(:baz)

      obj.baz
    end
  end
end
```

Running our first spec

Let's get started writing our first RSpec spec file before we delve deeper into the
concepts of the unit and the assertion. First, let's try an empty file. What will happen
if we create an empty file called `empty.rb` and try to run it as an RSpec spec file? On
a **POSIX (Portable Operating System Interface)** based operating system, such as
Linux or OS X, we could do the following:

We can see that RSpec correctly reports that there are no examples in the file. However, we also notice that RSpec reports that there are zero failures, which is, strictly speaking, correct. Finally, the last line shows the exit status of the `rspec empty.rb` command. An exit status of zero (`0`) indicates success on POSIX systems, which means that our empty test succeeded.

This seems a bit odd. There isn't a bug in RSpec, and we haven't made any typos. It's important to keep this simplest of cases in the back of our minds, even as we start building very complex specs. This empty test is useless and doesn't serve any purpose.

Let's move on to an actual spec file now. We'll create a file called `hello_world.rb` and put the following content in it:

```
require 'rspec'

describe 'hello world' do
  it 'returns true' do
    expect('hello world').to eq('hello world')
  end
end
```

Before we run this, let's have a look at what's in the file. Let's start from the inside out. The `expect` method declares an assertion, which is then specified with the `to` method together with the `eq` method. There are a number of matchers in RSpec, the most common of which is `eq`, which matches equality. Going out one layer, we see the `it` method, which is how we declare an example in RSpec. Finally, the `describe` method allows us to group one or more examples. We need to have at least one `describe` block and we can nest them in case of multiple blocks.

Now we'll run the spec and see what we get back:

```
● ● ●                          Terminal
$ rspec hello_world.rb

·

Finished in 0.00218 seconds (files took 0.13621 seconds to load)
1 example, 0 failures
$ echo $?
0
$ ▌
```

The spec passed again, and we see RSpec correctly detected that there was a single example in the file. The single dot on the first line of output looks odd when running a single spec, but it is a useful progress indicator when running a large number of specs, as there is one green dot for every passing spec and one red F for every failing test.

Now, let's add a failing spec to see what the output looks like. We'll create a new file called hello_and_bye.rb with the following content:

```
require 'rspec'

describe 'hello and bye' do
  it 'returns true' do
    expect('hello').to eq('hello')
  end

  it 'fails' do
    expect('bye').to eq('hello')
  end
end
```

Then we'll run the `rspec` command on it:

```
●  ●  ●                              Terminal
$ rspec hello_and_bye.rb
.F

Failures:

  1) hello and bye fails
     Failure/Error: expect('bye').to eq('hello')

       expected: "hello"
            got: "bye"

       (compared using ==)
     # ./hello_and_bye.rb:9:in `block (2 levels) in <top (required)>'

Finished in 0.00093 seconds (files took 0.08694 seconds to load)
2 examples, 1 failure

Failed examples:

rspec ./hello_and_bye.rb:8 # hello and bye fails
$ echo $?
1
$
```

This time we see that RSpec reports the failure, along with an explanation. We also notice that the exit status is no longer 0, but 1, which indicates failure. Any automated tools, such as continuous integration servers, would rely on that exit status to decide if our tests passed or failed, then react accordingly.

Now that we've seen some very rudimentary examples, let's remind ourselves of that first spec, the empty file. Are either `hello_world.rb` or `hello_and_bye.rb` any better than the empty file? Like the empty file, neither of these small spec files tests anything. We haven't even loaded any of our own code to test. But we've had to spend some effort to write the specs and haven't gotten anything in return. What's worse is that `hello_and_bye.rb` is failing, so we have to put in a little effort to fix it if we want our test suite to pass. Is there a point to fixing that failure?

These questions may seem absurd. However, developers writing tests will face such problems all the time. The question is, should we even write a test? The answer is not clear. The empty file represents that situation when we skip writing a test. The other two files represent cases where we've written useless tests, and where we have to spend time fixing a useless test in order to keep our test suite passing.

As we delve into RSpec, we will write specs that are very complex. Nevertheless, the fundamental issue will be exactly the same one that we faced with the empty file, `hello_world.rb`, and `hello_and_bye.rb`. We have to write tests that are useful and avoid wasting energy on writing and maintaining tests that don't serve a good purpose. The situation will be more nuanced, a matter of degrees of usefulness. But, in short, we should always consider the option of not writing a test at all!

Understanding the unit test

What is a **unit** of code? A unit is an isolated collection of code. A unit can be tested without loading or running the entire application. Usually, it is just a function. It is easy to determine what a unit is when dealing with code that is well organized into discrete and encapsulated modules. On the other hand, when code is splintered into ill-defined chunks that have cross-dependencies, it is difficult to isolate a logical unit.

What is a **test**? A test is code whose purpose is to verify other code. A single test case, (often referred to as an example in the RSpec community) consists of a set of inputs, one or more function calls, and an assertion about the expected output. A test case either passes or fails.

What is a **unit test**? It is an assertion about a unit of code that can be verified deterministically. There is an interdependency between the unit and the test, just as there is an interdependency between application code and test code. Finding the right unit and writing the right test go hand in hand, just as writing good application code and writing good test code go hand in hand. All of these activities occur as part of the same process, often at the same time.

Let's take the example of a simple piece of code that validates addresses. We could embed this code inside a `User` model that manages a record in a database for a user, like so:

```
Class User

  ...

  def save
    if self.address.street =~ VALID_STREET_ADDRESS_REGEX &&
       self.address.postal_code =~ VALID_POSTAL_CODE_REGEX &&
       CITIES.include?(self.address.city) &&
       REGIONS.include?(self.address.region) &&
       COUNTRIES.include?(self.address.country)

      DB_CONNECTION.write(self)
```

```
      true
    else
      raise InvalidRecord.new("Invalid address!")
    end
  end


  ...


  end
```

Writing unit tests for the preceding code would be a challenge, because the code is not modular. The separate concern of validating the address is intertwined with the concern of persisting the record to the database. We don't have a separate way to only test the address validation part of the code, so our tests would have to connect to a database and manage a record, or mock the database connection. We would also find it very difficult to test for different kinds of error, since the code does not report the exact validation error.

In this case, writing a test case for the single User#save method is difficult. We need to refactor it into several different functions. Some of these can then be grouped together into a separate module with its own tests. Finally, we will arrive at a set of discrete, logical units of code, with clear, simple tests.

So what would a good unit look like? Let's look at an improved version of the User#save method:

```
Class User


  def valid_address?
    self.address.street =~ VALID_STREET_ADDRESS_REGEX      &&
      self.address.postal_code =~ VALID_POSTAL_CODE_REGEX  &&
      CITIES.include?(self.address.city)                   &&
      REGIONS.include?(self.address.region)                &&
      COUNTRIES.include?(self.address.country)
  end

  def persist_to_db
    DB_CONNECTION.write(self)
  end

  def save
    if valid_address?
      persist_to_db
```

```
      true
    else
      false
    end
  end

  def save!
    self.save || raise InvalidRecord.new("Invalid address!")
  rescue
    raise FailedToSave.new("Error saving address: #{$!.inspect}")
  end

  ...

  end
```

Therefore, we write unit tests for two distinct reasons: first, to automatically test our code for correct behavior, and second, to guide the organization of our code into logical units.

Automated testing has evolved to include many categories of tests (for example, functional, integration, request, acceptance, and end-to-end). Sophisticated development methodologies have also emerged that are premised on automated verification, the most popular of which are TDD and BDD. The foundation for all of this is still the simple unit test. Code with good unit tests is good code that works. You can build on such a foundation with more complex tests. You can base your development workflow on such a foundation.

However, you are unlikely to get much benefit from complex tests or sophisticated development methodologies if you don't build on a foundation of good unit tests. Further, the same factors that contribute to good unit tests also contribute, at a higher level of abstraction, to good complex tests. Whether we are testing a single function or a complex system composed of separate services, the fundamental questions are the same. Is the assertion clear and verifiable? Is the test case logically coherent? Are the inputs and outputs precisely specified? Are error cases considered? Is the test readable and maintainable? Does the test often provide false positives (the test passes even though the system does not behave correctly) or false negatives (the test fails even though the system works correctly)? Is the test providing value, or is it more trouble than it's worth?

In summary, testing begins and ends with the unit test.

Writing specs with RSpec

We have discussed a lot of theory; now, let's start applying it. We'll write a few specs for the `AddressValidator` module defined below:

```ruby
module AddressValidator
  FIELD_NAMES = [:street, :city, :region, :postal_code, :country]
  VALID_VALUE = /^[A-Za-z0-9\.\# ]+$/
  class << self
    def valid?(o)
      normalized = parse(o)
      FIELD_NAMES.all? do |k|
        v = normalized[k]
        !v.nil? && v != "" && valid_part?(v)
      end
    end

    def missing_parts(o)
      normalized = parse(o)
      FIELD_NAMES - normalized.keys
    end

    private

    def parse(o)
      if (o.is_a?(String))
        values = o.split(",").map(&:strip)
        Hash[ FIELD_NAMES.zip(values) ]
      elseif (o.is_a?(Hash))
        o
      else
        raise "Don't know how to parse #{o.class}"
      end
    end

    def valid_part?(value)
      value =~ VALID_VALUE
    end
  end
end
```

We'll store the code above in a file called `address_validator.rb`. Let's start with a couple of simple tests in this chapter. In the next chapter, we'll explore a few different ways to expand and improve these tests, but for now we'll just focus on getting up and running with our first real RSpec tests.

We'll put the following code in a file called `address_validator_spec.rb` in the same folder as `address_validator.rb`:

```ruby
require 'rspec'
require_relative 'address_validator'

describe AddressValidator do
  it "returns false for incomplete address" do
    address = { street: "123 Any Street", city: "Anytown" }
    expect(
      AddressValidator.valid?(address)
    ).to eq(false)
  end

  it "missing_parts returns an array of missing required parts" do
    address = { street: "123 Any Street", city: "Anytown" }
    expect(
      AddressValidator.missing_parts(address)
    ).to eq([:region, :postal_code, :country])
  end
end
```

Now, let's run RSpec (make sure you have it installed already!) like this:

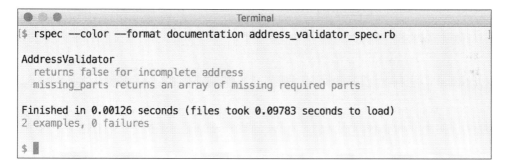

```
$ rspec --color --format documentation address_validator_spec.rb

AddressValidator
  returns false for incomplete address
  missing_parts returns an array of missing required parts

Finished in 0.00126 seconds (files took 0.09783 seconds to load)
2 examples, 0 failures

$
```

That's it. We used a couple of options to format the output, which is self-explanatory. We'll dig deeper into how to run specs with various options in future chapters. For now, we've accomplished our goal of running RSpec for a couple of unit tests.

Now is a good time to reflect on the concepts of testability and the unit of code. How testable is our `AddressValidator` module? Do you see any potential problems? What about the units we've tested? Are they isolated and modular? Do you see any places where we could do better? Take some time to review the code and think about these questions before moving on to the next section.

Test-driven development

It seems to make sense to write your code first and then to test it, as we did in our `AddressValidator` example above. Many people follow this approach. However, many others follow a process called TDD, where the tests are written first. Why do this? Let's take a brief aside before answering the question.

If you look at RSpec's official documentation, you will find that instead of the word `test`, the word `example` is used to describe the individual assertions to be found within the `it` block. Although it may appear less natural than `test`, in some ways `example` is more accurate. Automated tests rarely provide conclusive proof that a software system, or even just one of its functions, works. Most often, they contain a few test cases, which are nothing but examples of the code in action. Moreover, one of the main benefits of an automated assertion is to document the way the code behaves. Whereas `test` suggests a proof of correctness, `example` just suggests an instance of the code in action.

Coming back to the question of why someone would write their test before their code, we can apply the concept of the `example`. A methodical software engineer could benefit from documenting the code about to be written with some examples. Rather than adding these as comments in the code, the documentation can be written in the form of automated tests, or assertions. This way, as the code is being written, the tests can be run to give some feedback about how close, or how far, the code is to performing as initially expected.

If we refer to RSpec's home page, there is a link provided (`https://relishapp.com/rspec`), where we can read the following description:

> *RSpec is a Behaviour-Driven Development tool for Ruby programmers. BDD is an approach to software development that combines Test-Driven Development, Domain Driven Design, and Acceptance Test-Driven Planning. RSpec helps you do the TDD part of that equation, focusing on the documentation and design aspects of TDD.*

We see that TDD is mentioned, but the first sentence identifies RSpec with BDD. Although a definition is given, it refers to three other methodologies, leaving us perhaps with only a vague impression of some fancy approach to software development. So what is BDD really?

Behavior-driven development

BDD is an extension of the concepts of TDD to the complete functioning of a software system. Indeed, according to some proponents, BDD is a method for operating an entire organization!

Whereas TDD is concerned with tests and code, BDD is concerned with behaviors and benefits. BDD attempts to express the behavior of a system in plain, human language and justify the benefits that the behavior provides. TDD is written in code and does not attempt to justify the value of any part of the system. The loftiest vision of BDD is a methodology by which all features are specified and justified in clear human language, which can automatically be executed to verify that the system works as expected. Some other names sometimes used to refer to this lofty vision of BDD are **Specification by Example** and **executable documentation**.

If we look at our `AddressValidator` example, mentioned previously, we have an example of TDD. If we were to create a BDD-oriented specification for it, we may start with something like this:

```
Feature: Address Validation
  As a postal customer,
  In order to ensure my packages are delivered,
  I want to validate addresses

Scenario: Invalid address
  Given I enter "Seoul, USA"
  When I validate the address
  I should see the error message, "City and Country do not match"
```

This is the beginning of a **Cucumber** example. We won't go into Cucumber any further in this book, but it should be noted that RSpec is a closely related tool, and many of the developers who contribute to RSpec also contribute to Cucumber.

In the real world, the dividing line between TDD and BDD is not that clear. For most practical purposes, the only difference between TDD and BDD is in the style of the syntax used for expressions.

TDD leans more toward programmatic syntax, such as:

```
assert_equal(x, 5)
```

BDD, however, would use a syntax closer to human language, like RSpec's:

```
expect(x).to eq(5)
```

For the purposes of this book, we will strike a practical balance between TDD and BDD. Just by using RSpec, we are getting a hefty dose of BDD in our syntax. But we can still choose to structure our tests to follow the structure of our code (for example, having a single test for every function), which are nothing but unit tests. We can also choose to structure our tests according to high-level features, which is closer to BDD, or integration tests. In fact, we need to do a bit of both of these kinds of tests, as well as some tests that fall in between, which are sometimes called functional tests.

Summary

In this chapter, we have introduced the potential benefits and costs of automated testing, with a focus on the concept of testability, which we defined as the degree to which a system can be verified to work as expected. We learned about the importance of maintaining a positive balance between the benefits of testing and the cost of creating and maintaining tests. We then wrote a couple of simple unit tests and ran them with RSpec. Finally, we looked at different approaches to automated testing, from unit tests to TDD and BDD.

2
Specifying Behavior with Examples and Matchers

In this chapter, we'll see how RSpec's examples and matchers implement the general testing concepts of units and assertions. An example is the base unit for a set of RSpec specs and, within it, you must have a matcher to assert something, otherwise it would serve no purpose.

In this chapter, we will cover the following topics:

- Structure of a spec file
- RSpec output
- Matchers
- The `let` helper
- Testing for errors

Structure of a spec file

Let's look again at the `AddressValidator` module we introduced in *Chapter 1, Exploring Testability from Unit Tests to Behavior-Driven Development*, so we can understand its structure better. We'll also use some basic RSpec features to improve the tests. Let's look at the spec code:

```
require 'rspec'
require_relative 'address_validator'

describe AddressValidator do
  it "returns false for incomplete address" do
    address = { street: "123 Any Street", city: "Anytown" }
    expect(
```

```
      AddressValidator.valid?(address)
    ).to eq(false)
  end

  it "missing_parts returns an array of missing required parts" do
    address = { street: "123 Any Street", city: "Anytown" }
    expect(
      AddressValidator.missing_parts(address)
    ).to eq([:region, :postal_code, :country])
  end
end
```

We defined a local variable `address` in each example. This is fine for simple, one-off values. We could get the same functionality shared across multiple tests with a local function defined within the scope:

```
describe AddressValidator do
  def address
    { street: "123 Any Street", city: "Anytown" }
  end

  it "returns false for incomplete address" do
    expect(AddressValidator.valid?(address)).to eq(false)
  end

  it "missing_parts returns an array of missing required parts" do
    expect(
      AddressValidator.missing_parts(address)
    ).to eq([:region, :postal_code, :country])
  end
end
```

If the same value is used in more than one test, an instance variable in a `before` block can be used:

```
describe AddressValidator do

  # this block replaces the 'address' method
  before do
    @address = { street: "123 Any Street", city: "Anytown" }
  end

  it "valid? returns false for incomplete address" do
    expect(
      AddressValidator.valid?(@address)
```

```
    ).to eq(false)
  end

  it "missing_parts returns an array of missing required parts" do
    expect(
      AddressValidator.missing_parts(@address)
    ).to eq([:region, :postal_code, :country])
  end
end
```

In many cases, the object needs to change slightly from one test case to another. Local variables, local functions, or instance variables are tedious and make it hard to see the differences between test cases. For example, if we wanted to test for invalid characters in a city name, we would have the following:

```
describe AddressValidator do
  before do
    @address = { street: "123 Any Street", city: "Anytown" }
  end

  it "valid? returns false for incomplete address" do
    expect(AddressValidator.valid?(@address)).to eq(false)
  end

  it "missing_parts returns an array of missing required parts" do
    expect(
      AddressValidator.missing_parts(@address)
    ).to eq([:region, :postal_code, :country])
  end

  context "invalid characters in value" do
    before do
      # notice the value for :city includes special characters
      @address = { street: "123 Any Street", city: "Any$town%" }
    end

    it "invalid_parts returns keys with invalid values" do
      expect(
        AddressValidator.invalid_parts(@address)
      ).to eq([:city])
    end
  end
end
```

Using let and context

This scenario is very common, and inevitably will make the test harder to read, increasing the potential for misunderstanding the intent, which in turn will increase the likelihood of mistakes being made when the test or related code is changed. Before we see how to improve the test, we will learn about the `let` helper:

```
describe AddressValidator do
  let(:address) { {street: "123 Any Street", city: "Anytown"} }

  it "valid? returns false for incomplete address" do
    expect(AddressValidator.valid?(address)).to eq(false)
  end

  it "missing_parts returns an array of missing required parts" do
    expect(
      AddressValidator.missing_parts(address)
    ).to eq([:region, :postal_code, :country])
  end

  context "invalid characters in value" do

    let(:address){ {street: "123 Any Street", city: "Any$town%"} }

    it "invalid_parts returns keys with invalid values" do
      expect(
        AddressValidator.invalid_parts(address)
      ).to eq([:city])
    end
  end
end
```

The syntax is simple. The argument for the `let` helper is the name of the variable to be created, which you can reference within the same context as you would a local variable or function. In this case the argument is `:address`. The `let` helper also requires a block, that is is evaluated dynamically at runtime to provide the value for the object. In this case, we just supply a Hash for the value of `address`.

The secret to `let` is lambdas, or anonymous functions, which are evaluated at the moment they are called. Our first implementation doesn't show the power of lambdas. Using lambdas is what makes `let` so flexible and effective. Instead of a single, static `let` definition, we can create separate definitions for `street` and `city`, and reference them in `address`, allowing us to change individual parts of `address` as needed:

```
describe AddressValidator do
  let(:address) { { street: street, city: city } }
  let(:street)  { "123 Any Street"              }
  let(:city)    { "Anytown"                     }

  it "valid? returns false for incomplete address" do
    expect(AddressValidator.valid?(address)).to eq(false)
  end

  it "missing_parts returns an array of missing required parts" do
    expect(
      AddressValidator.missing_parts(address)
    ).to eq([:region, :postal_code, :country])
  end

  context "invalid characters in value" do
    let(:city) { "Any$town%" }

    it "invalid_parts returns keys with invalid values" do
      expect(
        AddressValidator.invalid_parts(address)
      ).to eq([:city])
    end
  end
end
```

Now we have a test case that clearly shows the differences in address, making the intent of the test case crystal clear. Using this pattern, we can add more cases with ease. We can change one or more nested values (for example city) or redefine address entirely:

```
describe AddressValidator do
  # notice that 'address' is defined as a Hash here
  let(:address) { { street: street, city: city } }
  let(:street)  { "123 Any Street"              }
  let(:city)    { "Anytown"                     }

  it "valid? returns false for incomplete address" do
    expect(AddressValidator.valid?(address)).to eq(false)
  end

  context "address contains invalid characters" do
    # here we've redefined 'address' to be a String
    let(:address) { "$123% A^ St., Anytown, CA, USA 12345" }
```

```
      it "valid? returns false for incomplete address" do
        expect(AddressValidator.valid?(address)).to eq(false)
      end
    end

    context "address is a String" do
      let(:address) { "123 Any St., Anytown" }

      it "valid? returns false for incomplete address" do
        expect(AddressValidator.valid?(address)).to eq(false)
      end
    end

    context "complete address" do
      # we define 'address' as a Hash, but with all values
      let(:address) do
        {
          street:      "123 Any Street",
          city:        "Anytown",
          region:      "Anyplace",
          country:     "Anyland",
          postal_code: "123456"
        }
      end

      it "valid? returns true" do
        expect(AddressValidator.valid?(address)).to eq(true)
      end

      context "address is a String" do
        let(:address) { "123 Any St., Anytown, CA, USA, 12345" }

        it "valid? returns true" do
          expect(AddressValidator.valid?(address)).to eq(true)
        end
      end
    end
  end
end
```

We've just seen how `let` is a simple but effective tool for organizing tests, making them easy to understand and to maintain. We've also started using `context` in order to organize our tests. In fact, `context` is just an alias for `describe`. Often, the outermost grouping of RSpec examples is defined with `describe` and the inner groups are grouped using `context`, but both are different names for the exact same function. In the cases we have seen, `context` gives us a local scope where we can define different versions of our test inputs with `let`.

Now, let's move on to matchers, which give us a flexible way of making assertions.

Matchers

We've been using RSpec's `eq` matcher to make assertions so far. We don't absolutely need this or any of RSpec's other matchers. We could use standard Ruby or define our own helper methods, like so:

```
describe 'no matchers' do
  it "valid? returns false for incomplete address" do
    expected = AddressValidator.valid?(address)
    if expected != false
      # RSpec's fail method allows us to manually fail an example
      fail "Expected #{expected} to have value of false"
    end
  end
end
```

There are a few problems with this approach. First, it is clumsy to write and read. Second, without a standard way of handling assertions, we're likely to wind up with a bunch of variations on the code above, making our output confusing. Finally, it is very easy to make mistakes with this kind of code, leading to invalid test results.

RSpec's matchers offer a simple and elegant syntax for making assertions. This makes it easy to write tests and also makes the intent of the test much clearer, allowing us to leverage our tests as documentation for our code.

Built-in matchers

We've used the `eq` matcher in many of our examples so far. RSpec comes with many other built-in matchers and allows us to define our own custom matchers as well. Some of the more common matchers are listed below (the full list can be found at http://www.relishapp.com/rspec/rspec-expectations/docs/built-in-matchers):

```
expect([]).to respond_to(:size)
expect([]).to be_empty
```

```
expect([].first).to be_nil
```

```
expect("foo bar").to match(/^f.+r$/)
expect([1,2]).to include(2)
expect([1,2,3]).to match_array([3,2,1])
```

Each example above is a successful assertion. We don't absolutely need any matchers except for eq, since we could rewrite any of the preceding assertions to use that instead, for example:

```
expect([1,2].include?(2)).to eq(true)
```

The various matchers offer us two main benefits. First, they make the tests much clearer and easier to understand. Second, they generate helpful error messages tailored to the specific situation. For example, compare the output from these two failing assertions:

```
expect([1,2,3].include?(4)).to eq(true)
# => expected: true
#         got: false

expect([1,2,3]).to include(4)
# => expected [1, 2, 3] to include 4
```

The first assertion's error message has no context at all, but the second one, which uses a specialized matcher, tells us exactly what the error is.

We can leverage this and make our testing much more effective by creating our own custom matchers for assertions that we use over and over. We'll learn how to do that in the following section.

Custom matchers

When a complex test assertion is used multiple times, it may be helpful to extract it into a custom matcher that can be reused. Let's say we have the following assertion:

```
expect(customer.discount_amount_for(product)).to eq(0.1)
```

This is a bit hard to read and the error message won't provide context. We could make it easier to read, like so:

```
actual = customer.discount_amount_for(product)
expect(actual).to eq(0.1)
```

To get a precise error message, we could do the following:

```
actual = customer.discount_amount_for(product)
if actual != 0.1
  fail "Expected discount amount to equal 0.1 not #{actual}"
end
```

However, what if we had a bunch of tests that had the same assertion? It would be tedious to redo all this for each test. More importantly, it is likely that each test case will have slight differences that are not easy to spot, allowing errors to slip in. RSpec's custom matchers allow us to encapsulate a custom assertion and error message, allowing us to write the following assertion:

```
expect(customer).to have_discount_of(0.1).for(product)
```

To make this work, we'll need to define a custom matcher. Actually, RSpec, by default, creates custom matchers for Boolean methods. For example, if we had the following spec, we could use the `have_discount_for` assertion:

```
expect(customer.has_discount_for?(product)).to eq(true)
```

```
expect(customer).to have_discount_for(product)
```

RSpec automatically matches `have_discount_for` to `has_discount_for?` by replacing `has` with `have` and removing the question mark. So custom matchers are a logical extension for cases where the assertion is more complex. In the case of `discount_amount_for`, we need to define a matcher that accepts an argument.

Let's work with code for an e-commerce site to find a user's discounts for a product. For example, a user may have earned a special discount by signing up for a promotion plan, or that product could be on sale for all users. We'll use a naïve implementation that we can run the specs against:

```
class Customer
  def initialize(opts)
    # assume opts = { discounts: { "a" => 0.1, "b" => 0.2 } }
    @discounts = opts[:discounts]
  end

  def has_discount_for?(product_code)
    @discounts.has_key?(product_code)
  end

  def discount_amount_for(product_code)
    @discounts[product_code] || 0
  end
end
```

We'd want a lot more from a real implementation, with maximum flexibility for defining simple and complex discounts based on customer attributes, product attributes, or any combination of the two. We'd need additional classes and modules to encapsulate behavior for products and the discounts themselves. The actual method that checks whether a customer has a discount may not be defined on the `Customer` class at all. It may be defined as `Product#discounted_for?(customer)` or `Discount#valid_for?(product, customer)`. We will return to the implementation details of the application code at the end of this section. The important thing to note is that we'll be able to use the same specs for different implementations by using custom matchers that can call the right method on the right class. Our goal here it to keep our specs logical and easy to read, regardless of implementation.

Let's start with a simple spec for the discount detection feature that will illustrate the use case for a custom matcher:

```
describe "product discount" do
  let(:product)      { "foo123"                        }
  let(:discounts)    { { product => 0.1 }              }
  subject(:customer) { Customer.new(discounts: discounts) }

  it "detects when customer has a discount" do
    actual = customer.discount_amount_for(product)
    expect(actual).to eq(0.1)
  end
end
```

Because the assertion uses the generic `eq` matcher, it is hard to read and easy to make mistakes. Also, when an assertion fails, we see a generic error message:

```
Failure/Error: expect(actual).to eq(0.1)
    expected: 0.1
         got: 0.2
```

This does not provide any meaningful context, forcing us to read the spec to figure out what went wrong.

Enhanced context in matcher output

We could write some extra code within the spec to give more context:

```
describe "product discount" do
  let(:product)      { "foo123"                        }
  let(:discounts)    { { product => 0.1 }              }
  subject(:customer) { Customer.new(discounts: discounts) }
```

```
     it "detects when customer has a discount" do
       actual = customer.discount_amount_for(product)
       if actual != 0.1
         fail "Expected discount amount to equal 0.1 not #{actual}"
       end
     end
   end
 end
```

This results in a better error message, but we had to generate it ourselves. Also, we would have to copy this code every time we wanted to make a similar assertion. There are a number of ways to make this spec easier to understand and maintain. We'll focus on using a custom matcher, which is a good fit for this scenario. Let's start with a very simple custom matcher and enhance it step by step:

```
require 'rspec/expectations'
RSpec::Matchers.define :be_discounted do |product, expected|
  match do |customer|
    customer.discount_amount_for(product) == discount
  end
end

describe "product discount" do
  let(:product)      { "foo123"                       }
  let(:discounts)    { { product => 0.1 }             }
  subject(:customer) { Customer.new(discounts: discounts) }

  it "detects when customer has a discount" do
    expect(customer).to be_discounted(product, 0.1)
  end
end
```

Now the test code is a lot simpler. RSpec now allows us to use the `be_discounted` matcher just like any of the built-in matchers (for example, `eq`, `eq(true)` and `have_key`).

We use `RSpec::Matchers.define` to create the custom matcher. The block arguments we pass to `RSpec::Matchers.define` are `name` and `discount`. These are the arguments we will pass to `be_discounted`. Within this block, we have access to a DSL that will allow us to specify the match criteria as well as other options. We use `match` with a block whose return value determines whether the assertion will pass (the block returns `true`) or fail (the block returns `false`). The block argument (`customer` in this case) is the value that we pass to `expect`; that is, the subject about which we are making an assertion.

When the spec fails, the error message will look like this:

```
Failure/Error: expect(customer).to be_discounted(product, 0.2)
  expected #<Customer:0x007f9d14df4bd0 @discounts={"foo123"=>0.1}> to
be discounted "foo123" and 0.2
```

This message looks messy, although it does include all of the context information about the customer, product, and discount. We can improve the error message by using `failure_message`, one of the DSL methods provided by `RSpec::Matchers`:

```
RSpec::Matchers.define :be_discounted do |product, discount|
  match do |customer|
    customer.discount_amount_for(product) == discount
  end

  failure_message do |customer|
    actual = customer.discount_amount_for(name)
    "expected #{product} discount of #{discount}, got #{actual}"
  end
end
```

Now a failing spec will provide us with the relevant info in a clean, organized format:

```
Failure/Error: expect(customer).to be_discounted(product, 0.2)
  expected foo123 discount of 0.2, got 0
```

We can simplify our matcher a bit by using an instance variable to store the actual value in the `match` block, and referencing it in `failure_message`:

```
RSpec::Matchers.define :be_discounted do |product, discount|
  match do |customer|
    @actual = customer.discount_amount_for(product)
    customer.discount_amount_for(product) == discount
  end

  failure_message do |actual|
    "expected #{product} discount of #{discount}, got #{actual}"
  end
end
```

Notice that `failure_message` now receives `@actual` as the block argument. Previously, `failure_message` received the `customer` object, but now that we've set an explicit value for `@actual` in `match`, it receives that new value instead of `customer`. Every DSL method in a custom matcher will always be called with the latest value of the `@actual` instance variable, which we set in this case to the value of the actual discount.

Creating a good custom error message

In this case, using an instance variable just helps us remove a line of duplication. For more complex matchers, however, instance variables can be very helpful in creating a good error message. Let's say we wanted to check for multiple discounts with a single assertion. Our error message would then need to show info for multiple mismatches:

```
RSpec::Matchers.define :be_discounted do |hsh|
  match do |customer|
    @customer = customer
    @actual   = hsh.keys.inject({}) do |memo, product, _|
      memo[product] = @customer.discount_amount_for(product)
      memo
    end

    differ = RSpec::Expectations::Differ.new

    @difference = differ.diff_as_object(hsh, @actual)
    @difference == "" # blank diff means equality
  end

  failure_message do |actual|
    "Expected #{@customer} to have discounts:\n"  +
    "  #{actual.inspect}.\n"                       +
    "Diff: "                                       +
    @difference
  end
end
```

To use this matcher, we could write a spec like this:

```
describe 'discounts' do
  let(:customer) { Customer.new }
  it 'is discounted by some amount' do
    expect(customer).to be_discounted('a', 0.1)
  end
end
```

Here we use `RSpec::Expectations::Differ` to give us a message with information on the differences between the actual and expected discounts, which are both instances of `Hash`. We store a reference to the customer object we pass to `expect` so that we can reference it in our failure message, which now looks like this:

```
Failure/Error: expect(customer).to be_discounted(discounts)
  Expected #<Customer:0x007fc592dcf550> to have discounts:
```

```
        {"a"=>0.2, "b"=>0.2, "c"=>0.2}.
Diff:
@@ -1,4 +1,4 @@
-"a" => 0.2,
-"b" => 0.2,
-"c" => 0.2
+"a" => 0.1,
+"b" => 0.1,
+"c" => 0.1
```

We can continue to improve our custom matcher. The assertion syntax we are using is a bit unnatural:

```
expect(customer).to be_discounted('a', 0.1)
```

We also used a `Hash` instead of two arguments:

```
expect(customer).to be_discounted('a' => 0.1, 'b' => 0.2)
```

But that was only to help pass in multiple discounts, and is not any more natural. What if we could use a natural syntax in which we specified the product and discount separately? RSpec has a built-in matcher, `be_within`, that works like this:

```
expect(1.5).to be_within(0.5).of(1.8)
```

A nice syntax for our custom matcher would be as follows:

```
expect(customer).to have_discount_of(0.1).for(product)
```

This is not hard to achieve. We simply need to define a plain Ruby class with the following methods:

- `matches?`
- `failure_message`
- `for`

We can then use an instance of this class along with a simple helper method to define our custom matcher:

```
class HaveDiscountOf
  def initialize(expected_discount)
    @expected = expected_discount
  end

  def matches?(customer)
    @actual = customer.discount_amount_for(@product)

    @actual == @expected
```

```
    end
    alias == matches? # only for deprecated customer.should syntax

    def for(product)
      @product = product
      self
    end

    def failure_message
      "expected #{@product} discount of #{@expected}, got #{@actual}"
    end
  end

describe "product discount" do
  # no need for the RSpec::Matchers.define DSL
  def have_discount_of(discount)
    HaveDiscountOf.new(discount)
  end

  let(:product)     { "foo123"                           }
  let(:discounts)   { { product => 0.1 }                 }
  subject(:customer) { Customer.new(discounts: discounts) }

  it "detects when customer has a discount" do
    expect(customer).to have_discount_of(0.1).for(product)
  end
end
```

Improving application code

Finally, let's get back to our application code. Now what if we changed our application code so that the actual check for a discount was done in a `product` class? We can simply alter the `match` block and keep the same specs:

```
RSpec::Matchers.define :be_discounted do |product, discount|
  match do |customer|
    product.discount_amount_for(customer) == discount
  end
end

describe "product discount" do
  let(:product)     { "foo123"                           }
  let(:discounts)   { { product => 0.1 }                 }
  subject(:customer) { Customer.new(discounts: discounts) }
```

```
    it "detects when customer has a discount" do
      expect(customer).to be_discounted(product, 0.1)
    end
  end
```

Actually, the implementation is arbitrary as long as our specs pass all the required information. We could encapsulate the entire check in a `Discount` class, perhaps following the Data, Context and Interaction (DCI) pattern (see `http://www.artima.com/articles/dci_vision.html`), like so:

```
  RSpec::Matchers.define :be_discounted do |product, expected|
    match do |customer|
      @discount = Discount.find(
        product:  product,
        customer: customer
      )
      @discount.amount == expected
    end
  end
```

The above would require some changes to our spec setup, but the actual assertion would be the same:

```
  describe "product discount" do
    let(:product)       { "foo123"    }
    let(:amount)        {   0.1       }
    subject(:customer) { Customer.new }

    before do
      Discount.create(
        product:  product,
        customer: customer,
        amount:   amount
      )
    end

    it "detects when customer has a discount" do
      expect(customer).to be_discounted(product, amount)
    end
  end
```

Putting it all together, we can not only improve our specs, but improve our application code so that the `Customer` class is orthogonal to (that is, has no knowledge of) the `Discount` class:

```ruby
class Customer
  # ... no discount info here!
end

class Discount
  attr_reader :amount, :customer, :product

  def initialize(opts={})
    @customer = opts[:customer]
    @product  = opts[:product]
    @amount   = opts[:amount]
  end

  STORE = []
  class << self
    def create(opts={})
      STORE << self.new(opts)
    end

    def find(opts={})
      STORE.select do |discount|
        opts.each do |k, v|
          discount.send(k) == v
        end
      end.first
    end
  end
end
```

Our final specs have only slightly changed and are clearer:

```ruby
class HaveDiscountOf
  def initialize(expected_discount)
    @expected = expected_discount
  end

  def matches?(customer)
    @actual = Discount.find(product: @product, customer: customer)
    @amt    = @actual && @actual.amount
    @amt == @expected
  end
  alias == matches? # only for deprecated customer.should syntax

  def for(product)
    @product = product
```

```
        self
    end

    def failure_message
      if @actual
        "Expected #{@product} discount of #{@expected}, got #{@amt}"
      else
        "#{@customer} has no discount for #{@product}"
      end
    end
end

describe "product discount" do
  def have_discount_of(discount)
    HaveDiscountOf.new(discount)
  end

  let(:product)      { "foo123"      }
  let(:amount)       { 0.1           }
  subject(:customer) { Customer.new }

  before do
    Discount.create(
      product:  product,
      customer: customer,
      amount:   amount
    )
  end

  it "detects when customer has a discount" do
    expect(customer).to have_discount_of(amount).for(product)
  end
end
```

We've developed some sophisticated custom matchers. However, we should keep in mind that this level of effort is not usually worth the benefit we get. The simpler custom matchers we started with will be seen much more often. Only when our application code is complex does it make sense to start considering sophisticated custom matchers like this, which, as we have just seen, not only ease our testing effort, but contribute to improving the modularity of our code.

So far, all of our tests have been testing success or failure. We haven't dealt at all with errors, which are extremely important to test for in any application.

Testing for errors

Tests are written to prevent errors from happening. The experienced programmer knows that errors are inevitable, and seeks to anticipate them by writing tests that deal specifically with errors.

There are three basic cases to deal with when testing errors:

- no error is raised
- an external error (an error class not in the code under test) is raised
- an internal error (a custom error class in the code under test) is raised

There are two basic decisions to make when writing code that raises an error.

The first is whether to allow an error to be raised or to attempt to recover from it with defensive practices, such as using a `rescue` block or fixing inputs that could cause an error to be raised. In general, lower-level, library code should expose errors without trying to recover from them, allowing the consumer of the code to handle error cases on their own. Higher-level application code should strive to recover from errors more aggressively, allowing only truly unrecoverable errors to be raised. For example, in a web application, we may have a page that retrieves the current weather using a `WeatherQuery` library that retrieves weather information from an HTTP service. If the HTTP service is unavailable, we will get an error when trying to retrieve weather information from it. The `WeatherQuery` class should raise an error to let us know something is wrong. And to avoid showing our end user an ugly error page, our application code, most likely the controller, should recover from the error by redirecting to the home page and displaying a friendly error message to the user.

The second decision to make is to determine when to create our own custom error classes instead of relying on errors raised by other code (defined in other parts of our code, an external gem, or the Ruby standard library). One good indicator of a need for custom classes is test code that checks for multiple existing errors. Often, many existing errors can be grouped together into a custom error that is more semantically meaningful. For example, in our example weather web app, we could anticipate a number of possible network-related errors, such as an unavailable network, a request timeout, unexpected response format, or missing data in the response, each of which would be a different error class. We can group all these errors into a custom `NetworkError` class, allowing consumers of the `WeatherQuery` class to handle a single error class, instead of requiring them to know about the internal implementation details of `WeatherQuery` so that they can handle the various errors that could be raised. In our controller, we would then only have to recover from `WeatherQuery::NetworkError`.

We'll start with the following `WeatherQuery` module, which provides weather forecasts using the `openweathermap.org` API:

```ruby
require 'net/http'
require 'json'
require 'timeout'

module WeatherQuery
  NetworkError = Class.new(StandardError)

  class << self
    def forecast(place)
      JSON.parse( http(place) )
    rescue JSON::ParserError
      raise NetworkError.new("Bad response")
    end

    private

    BASE_URI = 'http://api.openweathermap.org/data/2.5/weather?q='
    def http(place)
      uri = URI(BASE_URI + place)

      Net::HTTP.get(uri)
    rescue Timeout::Error
      raise NetworkError.new("Request timed out")
    rescue URI::InvalidURIError
      raise NetworkError.new("Bad place name: #{place}")
    rescue SocketError
      raise NetworkError.new("Could not reach #{uri.to_s}")
    end
  end
end
```

Our code anticipates network-related errors and can guarantee the user (the code that calls `WeatherQuery.forecast`) that either a valid response will be returned or a `WeatherQuery::NetworkError` will be raised. With this guarantee, the user doesn't have to worry about unexpected errors being raised by `WeatherQuery` due to network-related issues or problems with the `openweathermap.org` API service. How did we achieve this guarantee? First, we've extracted the network interactions into a private `http` method. Second, within this method, we've anticipated the different errors that could occur. We got this list through research as well as trial and error. Although the documentation for `Net::HTTP#get` states that it *never raises an exception*, the truth is that an exception will be raised in a number of common scenarios when the network request can't be made (for example, no response from the server, invalid URI, or network outage).

Now let's ensure that our guarantee is valid and test that, `WeatherQuery.forecast` will return valid data or raise a `WeatherQuery::NetworkError` exception.

To begin with, let's write a test to verify that a `WeatherQuery::NetworkError` is raised when a timeout occurs:

```
describe WeatherQuery do
  describe '.forecast' do
    it "raises a NetworkError instead of Timeout::Error" do
      expect(Net::HTTP).to receive(:get).and_raise(Timeout::Error)

      expected_error   = WeatherQuery::NetworkError
      expected_message = "Request timed out"

      expect{
        WeatherQuery.forecast("Antarctica")
      }.to raise_error(expected_error, expected_message)
    end
  end
end
```

We've used `and_raise` to mock the timeout and checked that the external timeout error is rescued and converted to an internal `WeatherQuery::NetworkError` using the `raise_error` matcher. That's all there is to it! This simple technique can add a new dimension to your specs and code. In fact, it is generally more important to write tests targeted at error cases than tests for the "happy path", since understanding your application's behavior in the event of exceptions is key to improving its robustness.

To test for exceptions being raised (or not raised), we used RSpec's `raise_error` matcher, which works with the block form of `expect`, as follows:

```
it "raises an error" do
  expect{ 1/0 }.to raise_error
  expect{ 1/0 }.to raise_error(ZeroDivisionError)
  expect{ 1/0 }.to raise_error(ZeroDivisionError, /divided/)
  expect{ 1/0 }.to raise_error(ZeroDivisionError, "divided by 0")

  expect{ 1/0 }.to raise_error do |e|
    expect(e.message).to eq("divided by 0")
  end
end

it "does not raise an error" do
  expect{
```

```
      1/1
    }.to_not raise_error
end
```

As you can see, you can match the expected error with as much precision as you like. For example, you can match any error, a specific class of error, an error message with a regular expression or exact match, as shown in the preceding code. You can also pass a block to `raise_error` for total control (in the case above, we check only for an error message regardless of class). One important point to note is that a negative assertion should only be used to assert that no error of any kind is raised. Why? Because checking that a specific kind of error has not been raised will very likely lead to false positives (see `https://github.com/rspec/rspec-expectations/issues/231`).

The error we've tested for the preceding code block, `ZeroDivisionError`, is easy to trigger. But many errors are not as easy to trigger. How would we recreate timeouts or network outages? We could try to write our own code that does this, but RSpec gives us the ability to mock errors using `and_raise`, as follows:

```
it "raises an error" do
  expect(Net::HTTP).to receive(:get).and_raise(Timeout::Error)

  # will raise Timeout::Error
  Net::HTTP.get('http://example.org')
end
```

The `and_raise` method allows us to specify the mock error with as much specificity as we like.

We'll also need a test that covers the case where JSON is not returned by the API, which commonly occurs when a server is down. Putting it all together, we have the following:

```
describe WeatherQuery do
  describe '.forecast' do
    context 'network errors' do
      let(:custom_error) { WeatherQuery::NetworkError }

      before do
        expect(Net::HTTP).to receive(:get)
                               .and_raise(err_to_raise)
      end

      context 'timeouts' do
        let(:err_to_raise) { Timeout::Error }
```

```ruby
    it 'handles the error' do
      expect{
        WeatherQuery.forecast("Antarctica")
      }.to raise_error(custom_error, "Request timed out")
    end
  end

  context 'invalud URI' do
    let(:err_to_raise) { URI::InvalidURIError }

    it 'handles the error' do
      expect{
        WeatherQuery.forecast("Antarctica")
      }.to raise_error(custom_error, "Bad place name: Antarctica")
    end
  end

  context 'socket errors' do
    let(:err_to_raise) { SocketError }

    it 'handles the error' do
      expect{
        WeatherQuery.forecast("Antarctica")
      }.to raise_error(custom_error, /Could not reach http:\/\//)
    end
  end
end

let(:xml_response) do
  %q(
    <?xml version="1.0" encoding="utf-8"?>
    <current>
      <weather number="800" value="Sky is Clear" icon="01n"/>
    </current>
  )
end

it "raises a NetworkError if response is not JSON" do
  expect(WeatherQuery).to receive(:http)
    .with('Antarctica')
    .and_return(xml_response)

  expect{
    WeatherQuery.forecast("Antarctica")
  }.to raise_error(
    WeatherQuery::NetworkError, "Bad response"
  )
end
end
end
```

We used the `and_return` method, which we haven't learned about yet. We'll cover that in depth in *Chapter 3, Taking Control of State with Doubles and Hooks*. All we need to know here is that we need it to prevent an actual HTTP request being made. Now we've covered every possible error case. We still have some choices to make about our overall design. If we pass a place name with a space to `WeatherQuery.forecast`, we'll get an error because the space is not URL-encoded. Should we detect bad input and raise an error before making the API request? Or should we try to handle spaces in the input by URL-encoding the input? Should we go further and add a validator to check the input for parsable formats and raise a new kind of error (for example, `WeatherQuery::UnparseablePlace`) if the input can't be parsed? I've chosen to keep the code simple by doing no validation or normalization of the input. This approach works when you can expect your users to be familiar with the workings of the backend API. If that expectation is not reasonable for your use case, then you should consider validation, normalization, or both.

What about the "happy path"? In this case, we have no tests for it, and we don't really need any. Our code in this case is designed as a simple pass-through to the API. We are not changing the input or the output from the API, except to convert the JSON response into a Ruby object. What about actually hitting the API service to make sure everything works? That is a good idea but outside the scope of unit testing, the focus of this chapter. It is a very bad idea to allow any network connections in unit tests, so this type of test can be done separately in integration tests, which we will cover in detail in *Chapter 5, Simulating External Services*.

Summary

In this chapter, we've covered a lot of material. We are ready now to use RSpec for all kinds of testing and to help improve the quality of our code. Let's recall the topics we discussed:

- Structure of a spec file
- RSpec output
- Matchers
- The `let` helper
- Testing for errors

In our last section, on errors, we used a mock to generate an error. In the next chapter, we'll go into great detail about how to set up our testing environment using mocks and hooks to simulate various test scenarios.

3

Taking Control of State with Doubles and Hooks

In this chapter, we'll learn how RSpec implements the general testing concepts of stubs, mocks, and spies with `double`. We'll start by implementing our own custom mocking method and use it to show off some fun tricks. This will help us understand how mocking works. We'll also appreciate the variety of mocking tools that RSpec offers after we implement one of our own. Then we'll learn how to use RSpec hooks to set up and tear down state related to our tests. Here is what we will cover in this chapter:

- The role of stubs, mocks, and spies in testing
- How to use RSpec's `double`
- Spying on methods and objects with `expect` and `to_receive`
- Setup and teardown with `before` and `after` hooks

Why mock?

A unit in a real-world software system interfaces with many other units, internal and external. To have focused, isolated tests, we must somehow manage these interactions with other units. There are a few options. One is to simply use the other unit, as in the normal operation of the software in production. This option has the advantage that we don't do anything different in our tests, as compared to real-world usage of the software. However, this approach has two drawbacks. First, it undermines our goal of isolated unit testing by tying the tests for one unit with the exercise of code in another unit. Second, it is often not practical to load and set up the other unit in our tests due to a complex setup, external dependencies, and increased runtime of the test.

A common approach to dealing with the problem of external interfaces in testing is to use a mock in place of the other unit. Given Ruby's dynamic nature, it is quite easy to implement such a feature by using `Module#define_method`. Here is a naïve implementation to demonstrate the basic concept:

```ruby
class Object
  def self.mock(method_name, return_value)
    klass = self

    # store existing method, if there is one, for restoration
    existing_method = if klass.method_defined?(method_name)
      klass.instance_method(method_name)
    else
      nil
    end

    klass.send(:define_method, method_name) do |*args|
      return_value
    end

    # execute the passed block with the mock in effect
    yield if block_given?
  ensure
    # restore klass to previous condition
    if existing_method
      klass.send(:define_method, method_name, existing_method)
    else
      klass.send(:remove_method, method_name)
    end
  end
end
```

Here is how we could use our `Object.mock` method to redefine how addition works, by mocking the return value of `Fixnum#+` to always return `5000` regardless of which numbers are being passed. Note that in Ruby, `2 + 2` is actually evaluated as `2.+(2)`; that is, the method named + called on the `Fixnum` instance 2 with an argument of 2:

```
● ● ●              03 — irb -r./simple_mock.rb — irb — ruby — 80×24
$ irb -r./simple_mock.rb
awesome_print loaded
irb(main):001:0> puts "2 + 2 = #{2 + 2}"
2 + 2 = 4
nil
irb(main):002:0> Fixnum.mock(:+, 5000) do
irb(main):003:1*   puts "2 + 2 = #{2 + 2}"
irb(main):004:1> end
2 + 2 = 5000
nil
irb(main):005:0> puts "2 + 2 = #{2 + 2}"
2 + 2 = 4
nil
irb(main):006:0> ▌
```

It's fun to redefine addition like this, but how would we use our mocks in a test? Let's look at an example where we have a `ShoppingCart` class that can calculate the total price of the products it contains, each of which is an instance of a `Product` class. The real-world functionality depends on a database query to retrieve the list of products, but we want to avoid hitting the database in the unit test for a simple method like `ShoppingCart#total_price`, and we can achieve this using our little mock method, like so:

```
require 'rspec'
require_relative 'simple_mock'

class ShoppingCart
  def total_price
    products.inject(0) do |sum, product|
      sum += product.price
    end
  end

  # ...
```

```
end

class Product
  # ...
end

RSpec.describe ShoppingCart do
  describe '#total_price' do
    it "returns the sum of the prices of all products" do
      num_products  = 22
      price         = 100
      cart          = ShoppingCart.new
      some_products = [Product.new] * num_products

      ShoppingCart.mock(:products, some_products) do
        Product.mock(:price, price) do
          expect(cart.total_price).to eq(num_products * price)
        end
      end
    end
  end
end
```

Our `Object.mock` method works very similarly to RSpec's `allow_any_instance_of` method, and we can use that to achieve the same result, like this:

```
context "using RSpec's allow_any_instance_of" do
  it "returns the sum of the prices of all products" do
    num_products  = 22
    price         = 100
    cart          = ShoppingCart.new
    some_products = [Product.new] * num_products

    expect_any_instance_of(ShoppingCart).to receive(:products)
      .and_return(some_products)

    allow_any_instance_of(Product).to receive(:price)
      .and_return(price)

    expect(cart.total_price).to eq(num_products * price)
  end
end
```

RSpec gives us nicer syntax and also handles the definition and removal of the mock in a much safer and more sophisticated way, accounting for the subtle and tricky behavior of Ruby when it comes to methods and scope.

Note that we use `expect_any_instance_of` for the `cart` object but `allow_any_instance_of` for the `product` objects. The `cart` object only receives one method call, whereas the `product` instance will receive 22 method calls. Had we used `expect_any_instance_of`, the test would have failed unless we specified the exact number of times the method should be called. Generally, it's better to use expect-based methods rather than allow-based methods in tests as they can catch unexpected behavior, but sometimes it is not worth the extra clutter, as in this case.

As we saw in this example, with a mock, we can bypass externalities like a database connection so that we can test only the code that interests us. One important thing to note is that this interaction with external systems is a common source of bugs, so if all of our tests used mocks, we would very likely miss some big problems with any part of our code that depended on an external system. Knowing when to use a mock, and when not to, is a subjective and difficult judgment to make. We will return to this question at the end of this chapter.

Mocks, stubs, and doubles

The word **mock** is generic. Often the words **stub**, **fake**, and **double** are used to mean the same thing. To be precise, we could make a distinction between mocks and stubs. A **mock** is a fake object that stands in the place of an actual object. A **stub** is a fake method that is executed in place of an actual method. In practice, the terms are used interchangeably. In fact, our `Object#mock` method should have been named `Object#stub` if we were being consistent.

RSpec uses the method `double` to handle mocking. This is aliased as `stub` and `mock`, which can be confusing, but these aliases are both deprecated, so you shouldn't use them. There is also a method called `spy`, which is a convenience method based on `double` that I encourage you to avoid. All of these are defined in **rspec-mocks**, RSpec's test double framework.

You can think of `double` as returning a dummy object. For very simple cases, we could simply use `Object.new` instead. For example, in our shopping cart test, we didn't do anything with the `Product` class, and we could just use a regular object instead, like so:

```
context "using Object.new" do
  it "returns the sum of the prices of all products" do
    num_products = 22
    price        = 100
```

```
        cart          = ShoppingCart.new
        product       = Object.new
        some_products = [product] * num_products

        expect(cart).to receive(:products)
          .and_return(some_products)

        allow(product).to receive(:price)
          .and_return(price)

        expect(cart.total_price).to eq(num_products * price)
      end
  end
```

Switching from this to RSpec's `double` is very easy:

```
  context "using RSpec's double" do
    it "returns the sum of the prices of all products" do
      num_products  = 22
      price         = 100
      cart          = ShoppingCart.new
      product       = double('Product', price: price)
      some_products = [product] * num_products

      expect(cart).to receive(:products)
        .and_return(some_products)

      expect(cart.total_price).to eq(num_products * price)
    end
  end
```

Note that we set the stub for the `price` method by passing a `Hash` as the second argument to `double`, which is just one of its many features.

Using hooks

When a unit test requires a few setup steps, we can just include those steps in the test case before our assertion. For example, we may want to create some entries in a database or configure a service before we execute a test.

When the setup is more complex, it can clutter the test case, making the intent of the test harder to understand while increasing the effort required to maintain the test code. Even if the setup steps are short, if they are repeated in many places, duplication of code can lead to similar problems.

It is common for a setup to require cleanup or teardown steps to ensure tests don't interfere with each other. For example, if we added a few records to a database in a setup phase, we want to remove those records so that subsequent tests start off with a clean environment. Again, we can simply include the teardown steps in the test case after our assertion. This poses even larger problems than setup, because in addition to the issues of clutter and lower maintainability, we also face the problem of the teardown step not being executed in the case of a failed assertion. This leads to a polluted environment for any tests that are executed afterwards, making test results unreliable.

RSpec's hooks allow us to deal with setup and teardown by defining hooks that run `before`, `after`, or `around` (that is, both `before` and `after`) one or more test cases.

For example, let's look again at the `WeatherQuery` class and consider how we would test one additional feature. We want to cache requests locally to avoid unnecessary HTTP requests. For example, the first time we retrieve the weather for a given city, we store the result so that the next time we want to know the weather there, we won't need to send an HTTP request to the API.

Testing this feature require us to set up a certain state first, where we have made several requests that have filled the cache with some information. We can mock out HTTP requests and other internals, but we want to actually perform multiple queries and then make an assertion, rather than mock a state when multiple queries had already been made. If we mock out the cache value in our tests, then there isn't much left to test. That's why we want to make some queries and ensure our caching works correctly.

Since we are targeting specific methods, this test is still a unit test. We can still use mocks to make our tests easier to write and more focused. However, we want to go through a set of setup steps to test that our code correctly caches, records, and counts requests.

Let's start with tests for the caching feature:

```
describe WeatherQuery do
  describe 'caching' do
    let(:json_response) do
      '{"weather" : { "description" : "Sky is Clear"}}'
    end

    it "stores results in local cache" do
      expect(WeatherQuery).to receive(:http).
                              once.
                              and_return(json_response)
```

```
      actual = WeatherQuery.send(:cache)
      expect(actual).to eq({})

      WeatherQuery.forecast('Malibu,US')

      actual = WeatherQuery.send(:cache)
      expect(actual.keys).to eq(['Malibu,US'])
      expect(actual['Malibu,US']).to be_a(Hash)
    end

    it "uses cached result in subsequent queries" do
      expect(WeatherQuery).to receive(:http).
                              once.
                              and_return(json_response)

      WeatherQuery.forecast('Malibu,US')
      WeatherQuery.forecast('Malibu,US')
      WeatherQuery.forecast('Malibu,US')
    end
  end
end
```

Our tests are not too complicated, but we already have some problems. When we run our tests, the second one fails with the following message:

```
1) WeatherQuery caching uses cached result in subsequent queries
   Failure/Error: expect(WeatherQuery).to receive(:http).once
     (WeatherQuery).http(any args)
         expected: 1 time with any arguments
         received: 0 times with any arguments
```

The second problem is that our test code is a bit tricky. To fix the first problem, our code is going to get even trickier! Our second test fails because the cache from our first test run is still there when we run the second test. We'll need to either add a teardown step to the first test, add a setup test to the second test, or use an uncached place for the second test. None of these is a good option, but let's go with adding a teardown step to the first test:

```
it "stores results in local cache" do
  expect(WeatherQuery).to receive(:http).
                          once.
                          and_return(json_response)

  actual = WeatherQuery.send(:cache)
  expect(actual).to eq({})
```

```
WeatherQuery.forecast('Malibu,US')

actual = WeatherQuery.send(:cache)
expect(actual.keys).to eq(['Malibu,US'])
expect(actual['Malibu,US']).to be_a(Hash)

# clear the cache
WeatherQuery.instance_variable_set(:@cache, nil)
end
```

Now both tests pass, but we'll have to add the cache-clearing line to any test that affects the cache, including our second test. Since we have to reach into the internals of our `WeatherQuery` module to clear the cache, this is especially bad. To resolve these issues, we can move the setup and teardown code into hooks.

Let's define a `before` hook to take care of the setup steps and an `after` hook for the teardown step:

```
describe WeatherQuery do
  describe 'caching' do
    let(:json_response) do
      '{"weather" : { "description" : "Sky is Clear"}}'
    end

    before do
      expect(WeatherQuery).to receive(:http).
                                once.
                                and_return(json_response)

      actual = WeatherQuery.send(:cache)
      expect(actual).to eq({})
    end

    after do
      WeatherQuery.instance_variable_set(:@cache, nil)
    end

    it "stores results in local cache" do
      WeatherQuery.forecast('Malibu,US')

      actual = WeatherQuery.send(:cache)
      expect(actual.keys).to eq(['Malibu,US'])
      expect(actual['Malibu,US']).to be_a(Hash)
    end
```

```
      it "uses cached result in subsequent queries" do
        WeatherQuery.forecast('Malibu,US')
        WeatherQuery.forecast('Malibu,US')
        WeatherQuery.forecast('Malibu,US')
      end
    end
  end
```

Now our tests are much clearer. The setup and teardown steps are clearly separated from the test cases and everything is easier to understand and maintain. If we want to add new test cases, we don't have to worry about setup or teardown. Let's say we have an optional second parameter which allows us to disable caching by passing `false`. We can add a test for this as follows:

```
context "skip cache" do
  before do
    expect(WeatherQuery).to receive(:http).
                            with('Beijing,CN').
                            and_return(json_response)

    expect(WeatherQuery).to receive(:http).
                            with('Delhi,IN').
                            and_return(json_response)
  end

  it "hits API when false passed as second argument" do
    WeatherQuery.forecast('Malibu,US') # uses cache
    WeatherQuery.forecast('Beijing,CN', false)
    WeatherQuery.forecast('Delhi,IN', false)

    actual = WeatherQuery.send(:cache).keys
    expect(actual).to eq(['Malibu,US'])
  end
end
```

In this test, we've defined a second `before` block to do some additional setup. This second block will be executed in addition to the previously defined `before` block in the outer block. The outer `after` block will also be executed, so we can be sure to have a clean slate for any additional tests we write in the nested context.

What does `WeatherQuery` now look like? It's not that much different from what we had at the end of the *Testing for errors* section of *Chapter 2, Specifying Behavior with Examples and Matchers*:

```ruby
require 'net/http'
require 'json'
require 'timeout'

module WeatherQuery
  extend self

  class NetworkError < StandardError
  end

  def forecast(place, use_cache=true)
    if use_cache
      cache[place] ||= JSON.parse( http(place) )
    else
      JSON.parse( http(place) )
    end
  rescue JSON::ParserError
    raise NetworkError.new("Bad response")
  end

  private

  def cache
    @cache ||= {}
  end

  BASE_URI = 'http://api.openweathermap.org/data/2.5/weather?q='
  def http(place)
    uri = URI(BASE_URI + place)

    Net::HTTP.get(uri)
  rescue Timeout::Error
    raise NetworkError.new("Request timed out")
  rescue URI::InvalidURIError
    raise NetworkError.new("Bad place name: #{place}")
  rescue SocketError
    raise NetworkError.new("Could not reach #{uri.to_s}")
  end
end
```

We've added a second parameter, `use_cache`, which defaults to `true`. If this second parameter is set to `false`, then our code does no caching at all. To handle caching, we've added a private method, `cache`, to handle access to an instance variable `@cache`, which is an empty `Hash` by default. When `use_cache` is true, we use **memoization** (`||=`) to check and set the value for `cache` in one line. We first check for an existing cache value for the given place. If we have a key defined for the place, then we simply return the value from the cache. If there is no value in the cache for the place, we perform the HTTP request, parse the JSON, set the value in cache with the place as the key, and then return the value.

Controlling when hooks are executed

Both `before` and `after` accept an argument, which can be `:suite`, `:context`, or `:example`. The default value is `:example`, so when we defined the `before` block in our tests above, we were actually defining a `before(:example)` block. Similarly, our `after` block was actually an `after(:example)` block. This means that the block is executed before (or after) each test case in the context where it is defined. This is most often the desired behavior for hooks. However, there are cases when setup and teardown are not required after each test. Usually, to improve performance, in those cases you can set the hook to run before the context where it is defined, or before the entire test suite.

There is also an `around` block (which also accepts an argument of `:suite`, `:context`, or `:example`) that can be used to define a single block that does both setup and teardown. I prefer to usually keep setup and teardown separate. Also, `around` hooks do not have access to the test context like `before` and `after` hooks, so you can't do mocking or set expectations in an `around` hook, though you can make assertions.

In our example, we set an expectation that we would receive an HTTP request in the `before` hook (and returned a mock JSON response). That would not work in an `around` hook. We also cleared the cache in our `after` hook. This code would work fine in an `around` hook. If we were to use an `around` hook, we would have something such as the following:

```
around(:each) do |example|
  actual = WeatherQuery.send(:cache)
  expect(actual).to eq({})

  example.run

  WeatherQuery.instance_variable_set(:@cache, nil)
end
```

Using the code above would make actual HTTP requests, unless we mocked that out elsewhere. Generally, `around` hooks are useful if you are doing advanced state management in your tests. You can control which examples are run based on arbitrary criteria. You also have access to RSpec metadata about an example and can use that to set different expectations. I advise against using `around` hooks because they enable very complex tests. Of course, there is an exception to every rule, so there may be cases when an `around` hook is a good option. But I strongly urge you to explore alternatives first and, if you do use `around` hooks, make sure to fully understand what is happening inside your hook.

Advanced state control with hooks and mocks

Let's delve deeper into hooks and mocks. There are at least two related features that would be nice to have in `WeatherQuery`:

- Store and retrieve a history of weather queries
- Keep a count of the total number of API requests sent so we can throttle usage to avoid flooding the API with too many requests

As you can see, both of these features require us to set up a certain state before we can test them. In this case, we want to avoid mocking the actual state changes, because we would then have little or nothing to test. We can mock HTTP requests and other details not related to the state change, but we want to actually perform multiple queries and then make an assertion, rather than mock a state when multiple queries have been made. For example, if we are testing a method such as `WeatherQuery.api_request_count` without actually making requests, we would mock an instance variable (or other internal counter store) and check that the method returned the mock value we set, but then we're testing very little. Or, we could do a single request and check that the internal counter was incremented by one, but then our test case is too simplistic to give us much confidence that our code will work when many requests are made. We want to test that the internal counter is updated correctly under normal usage conditions, so using mocks in this case is not helpful.

Let's test the history feature first:

```
describe WeatherQuery do
  describe 'query history' do
    before do
      expect(WeatherQuery.history).to eq([])
      allow(WeatherQuery).to receive(:http).and_return("{}")
    end
```

```ruby
    after do
      WeatherQuery.instance_variable_set(:@history, nil)
    end

    it "stores every place requested" do
      places = %w(
        Malibu,US
        Beijing,CN
        Delhi,IN
        Malibu,US
        Malibu,US
        Beijing,CN
      )

      places.each {|s| WeatherQuery.forecast(s) }

      expect(WeatherQuery.history).to eq(places)
    end

    it "does not allow history to be modified" do
      expect {
        WeatherQuery.history = ['Malibu,CN']
      }.to raise_error

      expect(WeatherQuery.history).to eq([])
    end
  end
end
```

This is not that different from our tests for the caching feature. The `history` method is public since we want to make this available, but we also want to make sure it is read-only. Our `before` block now uses `allow` instead of `expect` to mock HTTP requests, so we don't have to specify how many times the `http` method will be called, since that is not a concern of this test. We are clearing out the `@history` instance variable here instead of `@cache`. Keep in mind that caching is still in effect and the cache set in the first test is still there in the second test. Our tests pass, but we have polluted the cache for any subsequent tests. We could also clear the cache in our `after` block, but that approach can be troublesome as we are not even dealing with `cache` in these tests.

If we have to know about all the internal state mechanisms of our code in every test, then we are going to have some ugly test code which is liable to give us false results. In this case, we can solve the problem by adding a helper method to our `WeatherQuery` tests to clear all internal state. We could also add the method to `WeatherQuery` itself. Generally, it's better to add this type of code to the application itself if it could be of potential use. We know that we won't be able to keep infinitely long caches or history, so we will need a way to clear those from time to time. So, let's add a `clear!` method to `WeatherQuery` to handle clearing of all internal state. Now our `after` hook becomes the following:

```
after do
  WeatherQuery.clear!
end
```

We can be assured we are not polluting subsequent tests.

Now on to the count of API requests. This is separate from the history feature, as we only want to track API requests, whereas `history` should keep track of all queries, including cached ones. We'll figure out the implementation later. First let's write the tests for it:

```
describe WeatherQuery do
  describe 'number of API requests' do
    before do
      WeatherQuery.clear!

      expect(WeatherQuery.api_request_count).to eq(0)
      allow(WeatherQuery).to receive(:http).and_return("{}")
    end

    after do
      WeatherQuery.clear!
    end

    it "stores every place requested" do
      places = %w(
        Malibu,US
        Beijing,CN
        Delhi,IN
        Malibu,US
        Malibu,US
        Beijing,CN
      )

      places.each {|s| WeatherQuery.forecast(s) }
```

```
      expect(WeatherQuery.api_request_count).to eq(3)
    end

    it "does not allow count to be modified" do
      expect {
        WeatherQuery.api_request_count = 100
      }.to raise_error

      expect {
        WeatherQuery.api_request_count += 10
      }.to raise_error

      expect(WeatherQuery.api_request_count).to eq(0)
    end
  end
end
```

Notice that our hooks are almost the same and we can assume that our new `WeatherQuery.clear!` method will take care of cleaning up any internal state related to the `api_request_count` method. Now, what does `WeatherQuery` look like with all these new features? It looks like this:

```ruby
require 'net/http'
require 'json'
require 'timeout'

module WeatherQuery
  extend self

  NetworkError = Class.new(StandardError)

  def forecast(place, use_cache=true)
    add_to_history(place)

    if use_cache
      cache[place] ||= begin
        @api_request_count += 1
        JSON.parse( http(place) )
      end
    else
      JSON.parse( http(place) )
    end
  rescue JSON::ParserError
    raise NetworkError.new("Bad response")
  end
```

```ruby
  def api_request_count
    @api_request_count ||= 0
  end

  def history
    (@history || []).dup
  end

  def clear!
    @history           = []
    @cache             = {}
    @api_request_count = 0
  end

  private

  def add_to_history(s)
    @history ||= []
    @history << s
  end

  def cache
    @cache ||= {}
  end

  BASE_URI = 'http://api.openweathermap.org/data/2.5/weather?q='
  def http(place)
    uri = URI(BASE_URI + place)

    Net::HTTP.get(uri)
  rescue Timeout::Error
    raise NetworkError.new("Request timed out")
  rescue URI::InvalidURIError
    raise NetworkError.new("Bad place name: #{place}")
  rescue SocketError
    raise NetworkError.new("Could not reach #{uri.to_s}")
  end
end
```

There's plenty more we could do. For example, we might want to measure the number of API requests in the past hour to prevent spikes in usage. Actually, the request count is not that useful without a time component. To test this, we'd need to simulate the passage of time. We may want our history to store more information for each query besides just the place. We might want to add support for multiple service providers as well as authentication. All of these advanced features will require state management in our tests, and we'll need to use hooks to make our tests maintainable and reliable.

Summary

In this chapter, we learned about RSpec's mocks, which let us change how specific parts of our code behave during tests. We also learned about hooks, which we used to set up and tear down state for our test cases. Using these tools, we learned how to test complex stateful behavior in our application code, which we also adjusted to increase testability.

4
Setting Up and Cleaning Up

This chapter discusses support code to set tests up and clean up after them. Initialization, configuration, cleanup, and other support code related to RSpec specs are important in real-world RSpec usage. We will learn how to cleanly organize support code in real-world applications by learning about the following topics:

- Configuring RSpec with `spec_helper.rb`
- Initialization and configuration of resources
- Preventing tests from accessing the Internet with **WebMock**
- Maintaining clean test state
- Custom helper code
- Loading support code on demand with tags

Configuring RSpec with spec_helper.rb

The RSpec specs that we've seen so far have functioned as standalone units. Specs in the real world, however, almost never work without supporting code to prepare the test environment before tests are run and ensure it is cleaned up afterwards. In fact, the first line of nearly every real-world RSpec spec file loads a file that takes care of initialization, configuration, and cleanup:

```
require 'spec_helper'
```

By convention, the entry point for all support code for specs is in a file called `spec_helper.rb`. Another convention is that specs are located in a folder called `spec` in the root folder of the project. The `spec_helper.rb` file is located in the root of this `spec` folder.

Now that we know where it goes, what do we actually put in `spec_helper.rb`? Let's start with an example:

```
# spec/spec_helper.rb
require 'rspec'

RSpec.configure do |config|
  config.order            = 'random'
  config.profile_examples = 3
end
```

To see what these two options do, let's create a couple of dummy spec files that include our `spec_helper.rb`. Here's the first spec file:

```
# spec/first_spec.rb
require 'spec_helper'

describe 'first spec' do
  it 'sleeps for 1 second' do
    sleep 1
  end

  it 'sleeps for 2 seconds' do
    sleep 2
  end

  it 'sleeps for 3 seconds' do
    sleep 3
  end
end
```

And here's our second spec file:

```
# spec/second_spec.rb
require 'spec_helper'

describe 'second spec' do
  it 'sleeps for 4 second' do
    sleep 4
  end

  it 'sleeps for 5 seconds' do
    sleep 5
  end

  it 'sleeps for 6 seconds' do
```

```
    sleep 6
  end
end
```

Now let's run our two spec files and see what happens:

```
●  ●  ●                              Terminal
$ rspec spec --format documentation

Randomized with seed 8669

second spec
  sleeps for 5 seconds
  sleeps for 4 second
  sleeps for 6 seconds

first spec
  sleeps for 2 seconds
  sleeps for 1 second
  sleeps for 3 seconds

Top 3 slowest examples (15.01 seconds, 71.4% of total time):
  second spec sleeps for 6 seconds
    6 seconds ./spec/second_spec.rb:12
  second spec sleeps for 5 seconds
    5.01 seconds ./spec/second_spec.rb:8
  second spec sleeps for 4 second
    4 seconds ./spec/second_spec.rb:4

Top 2 slowest example groups:
  second spec
    5 seconds average (15.01 seconds / 3 examples) ./spec/second_spec.rb:3
  first spec
    2 seconds average (6.01 seconds / 3 examples) ./spec/first_spec.rb:3

Finished in 21.03 seconds (files took 0.09176 seconds to load)
6 examples, 0 failures

Randomized with seed 8669

$ ▊
```

We note that we used `--format documentation` when running RSpec so that we see
the order in which the tests were run (the default format just outputs a green dot for
each passing test). From the output, we can see that the tests were run in a random
order. We can also see the three slowest specs.

Although this was a toy example, I would recommend using both of these configuration options for RSpec. Running examples in a random order is very important, as it is the only reliable way of detecting bad tests which sometimes pass and sometimes fail based on the order that the overall test suite is run. Also, keeping tests running fast is very important for maintaining a productive development flow, and seeing which tests are slow on every test run is the most effective way of encouraging developers to make the slow tests fast, or remove them from the test run.

We'll return to both test order and test speed later. For now, let us just note that RSpec configuration is very important to keeping our specs reliable and fast.

Initialization and configuration of resources

Real-world applications rely on resources, such as databases, and external services, such as HTTP APIs. These must be initialized and configured for the application to work properly. When writing tests, dealing with these resources and services can be a challenge because of two opposing fundamental interests.

First, we would like the test environment to match as closely as possible the production environment so that tests that interact with resources and services are realistic. For example, we may use a powerful database system in production that runs on many servers to provide the best performance. Should we spend money and effort to create and maintain a second production-grade database environment just for testing purposes?

Second, we would like the test environment to be simple and relatively easy to understand, so that we understand what we are actually testing. We would also like to keep our code modular so that components can be tested in isolation, or in simpler environments that are easier to create, maintain, and understand. If we think of the example of the system that relies on a database cluster in production, we may ask ourselves whether we are better off using a single-server setup for our test database. We could even go so far as to use an entirely different database for our tests, such as the file-based SQLite.

As always, there are no easy answers to such trade-offs. The important thing is to understand the costs and benefits, and adjust where we are on the continuum between production faithfulness and test simplicity as our system evolves, along with the goals it serves. For example, for a small hobbyist application or a project with a limited budget, we may choose to completely favor test simplicity. As the same code grows to become a successful fan site or a big-budget project, we may have a much lower tolerance for failure, and have both the motivation and resources to shift towards production faithfulness for our test environment.

Some rules of thumb to keep in mind:

- Unit tests are better places for test simplicity
- Integration tests are better places for production faithfulness
- Try to cleverly increase production faithfulness in unit tests
- Try to cleverly increase test simplicity in integration tests
- In between unit and integration tests, be clear what is and isn't faithful to the production environment

A case study of test simplicity with an external service

Let's put these ideas into practice, drawing on the `WeatherQuery` code we worked with in *Chapter 3, Taking Control of State with Doubles and Hooks*. I haven't changed the application code, except to rename the module `OldWeatherQuery`. The test code is also slightly changed to require a `spec_helper` file and to use a `subject` block to define an alias for the module name, which makes it easier to rename the code without having to change many lines of test code.

So let's look at our three files now. First, here's the application code:

```
# old_weather_query.rb

require 'net/http'
require 'json'
require 'timeout'

module OldWeatherQuery
  extend self

  class NetworkError < StandardError
  end

  def forecast(place, use_cache=true)
    add_to_history(place)

    if use_cache
      cache[place] ||= begin
        @api_request_count += 1
        JSON.parse( http(place) )
      end
    else
```

```ruby
      JSON.parse( http(place) )
    end
  rescue JSON::ParserError
    raise NetworkError.new("Bad response")
  end

  def api_request_count
    @api_request_count ||= 0
  end

  def history
    (@history || []).dup
  end

  def clear!
    @history          = []
    @cache            = {}
    @api_request_count = 0
  end

  private

  def add_to_history(s)
    @history ||= []
    @history << s
  end

  def cache
    @cache ||= {}
  end

  BASE_URI = 'http://api.openweathermap.org/data/2.5/weather?q='
  def http(place)
    uri = URI(BASE_URI + place)

    Net::HTTP.get(uri)
  rescue Timeout::Error
    raise NetworkError.new("Request timed out")
  rescue URI::InvalidURIError
    raise NetworkError.new("Bad place name: #{place}")
  rescue SocketError
    raise NetworkError.new("Could not reach #{uri.to_s}")
  end
end
```

Next is the spec file:

```
# spec/old_weather_query_spec.rb

require_relative 'spec_helper'
require_relative '../old_weather_query'

describe OldWeatherQuery do
  subject(:weather_query) { described_class }

  describe 'caching' do
    let(:json_response) do
      '{"weather" : { "description" : "Sky is Clear"}}'
    end

    around(:example) do |example|
      actual = weather_query.send(:cache)
      expect(actual).to eq({})

      example.run

      weather_query.clear!
    end

    it "stores results in local cache" do
      weather_query.forecast('Malibu,US')

      actual = weather_query.send(:cache)
      expect(actual.keys).to eq(['Malibu,US'])
      expect(actual['Malibu,US']).to be_a(Hash)
    end

    it "uses cached result in subsequent queries" do
      weather_query.forecast('Malibu,US')
      weather_query.forecast('Malibu,US')
      weather_query.forecast('Malibu,US')
    end
  end

  describe 'query history' do
    before do
      expect(weather_query.history).to eq([])
      allow(weather_query).to receive(:http).and_return("{}")
    end
```

```ruby
  after do
    weather_query.clear!
  end

  it "stores every place requested" do
    places = %w(
      Malibu,US
      Beijing,CN
      Delhi,IN
      Malibu,US
      Malibu,US
      Beijing,CN
    )

    places.each {|s| weather_query.forecast(s) }

    expect(weather_query.history).to eq(places)
  end

  it "does not allow history to be modified" do
    expect {
      weather_query.history = ['Malibu,CN']
    }.to raise_error

    weather_query.history << 'Malibu,CN'
    expect(weather_query.history).to eq([])
  end
end

describe 'number of API requests' do
  before do
    expect(weather_query.api_request_count).to eq(0)
    allow(weather_query).to receive(:http).and_return("{}")
  end

  after do
    weather_query.clear!
  end

  it "stores every place requested" do
    places = %w(
```

```
        Malibu,US
        Beijing,CN
        Delhi,IN
        Malibu,US
        Malibu,US
        Beijing,CN
      )

      places.each {|s| weather_query.forecast(s) }

      expect(weather_query.api_request_count).to eq(3)
    end

    it "does not allow count to be modified" do
      expect {
        weather_query.api_request_count = 100
      }.to raise_error

      expect {
        weather_query.api_request_count += 10
      }.to raise_error

      expect(weather_query.api_request_count).to eq(0)
    end
  end
end
```

And last but not least, our spec helper file, which has also changed only slightly: we only configure RSpec to show one slow spec (to keep test results uncluttered) and use color in the output to distinguish passes and failures more easily:

```
# spec/spec_helper.rb

require 'rspec'

RSpec.configure do |config|
  config.order            = 'random'
  config.profile_examples = 1
  config.color            = true
end
```

When we run these specs, something unexpected happens. Most of the time the specs pass, but sometimes they fail. If we keep running the specs with the same command, we'll see the tests pass and fail apparently at random. These are flaky tests, and we have exposed them because of the random order configuration we chose. If our tests run in a certain order, they fail. The problem could be simply in our tests. For example, we could have forgotten to clear state before or after a test. However, there could also be a problem with our code. In any case, we need to get to the bottom of the situation:

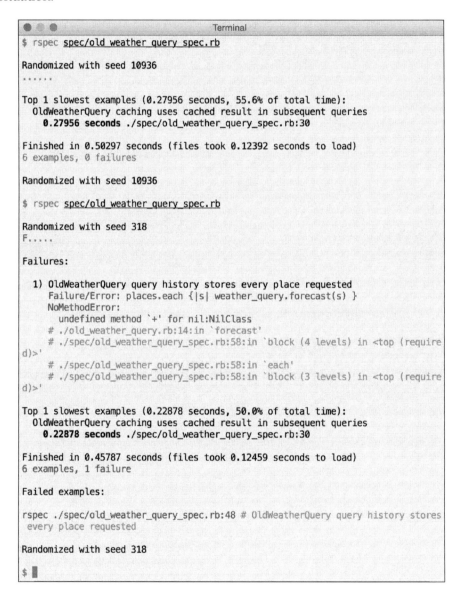

```
                              Terminal
$ rspec spec/old_weather_query_spec.rb

Randomized with seed 10936
.......

Top 1 slowest examples (0.27956 seconds, 55.6% of total time):
  OldWeatherQuery caching uses cached result in subsequent queries
    0.27956 seconds ./spec/old_weather_query_spec.rb:30

Finished in 0.50297 seconds (files took 0.12392 seconds to load)
6 examples, 0 failures

Randomized with seed 10936

$ rspec spec/old_weather_query_spec.rb

Randomized with seed 318
F.....

Failures:

  1) OldWeatherQuery query history stores every place requested
     Failure/Error: places.each {|s| weather_query.forecast(s) }
     NoMethodError:
       undefined method `+' for nil:NilClass
     # ./old_weather_query.rb:14:in `forecast'
     # ./spec/old_weather_query_spec.rb:58:in `block (4 levels) in <top (require
d)>'
     # ./spec/old_weather_query_spec.rb:58:in `each'
     # ./spec/old_weather_query_spec.rb:58:in `block (3 levels) in <top (require
d)>'

Top 1 slowest examples (0.22878 seconds, 50.0% of total time):
  OldWeatherQuery caching uses cached result in subsequent queries
    0.22878 seconds ./spec/old_weather_query_spec.rb:30

Finished in 0.45787 seconds (files took 0.12459 seconds to load)
6 examples, 1 failure

Failed examples:

rspec ./spec/old_weather_query_spec.rb:48 # OldWeatherQuery query history stores
 every place requested

Randomized with seed 318

$
```

We first notice that at the end of the failing test run, RSpec tells us `"Randomized with seed 318"`. We can use this information to run the tests in the order that caused the failure and start to debug and diagnose the problem. We do this by passing the `--seed` parameter with the value `318`, as follows:

```
$ rspec spec/old_weather_query_spec.rb --seed 318
```

The problem has to do with the way that we increment `@api_request_count` without ensuring it has been initialized. Looking at our code, we notice that the only place we initialize `@api_request_count` is in `OldWeatherQuery.api_request_count` and `OldWeatherQuery.clear!`. If we don't call either of these methods first, then `OldWeatherQuery.forecast`, the main method in this module, will always fail. Our tests sometimes pass because our setup code calls one of these methods first when tests are run in a certain order, but that is not at all how our code would likely be used in production. So basically, our code is completely broken, but our specs pass (sometimes). Based on this, we can create a simple spec that will always fail:

```
describe 'api_request is not initialized' do
  it "does not raise an error" do
    weather_query.forecast('Malibu,US')
  end
end
```

At least now our tests fail deterministically. But this is not the end of our troubles with these specs. If we run our tests many times with the seed value of `318`, we will start seeing a second failing test case that is even more random than the first. This is an `OldWeatherQuery::NetworkError` and it indicates that our tests are actually making HTTP requests to the Internet! Let's do an experiment to confirm this. We'll turn off our Wi-Fi access, unplug our Ethernet cables, and run our specs. When we run our tests without any Internet access, we will see three errors in total. One of them is the error with the uninitialized `@api_request_count` instance variable, and two of them are instances of `OldWeatherQuery::NetworkError`, which confirms that we are indeed making real HTTP requests in our code.

What's so bad about making requests to the Internet? After all, the test failures are indeed very random and we had to purposely shut off our Internet access to replicate the errors. Flaky tests are actually the least of our problems. First, we could be performing destructive actions that affect real systems, accounts, and people! Imagine if we were testing an e-commerce application that charged customer credit cards by using a third-party payment API via HTTP. If our tests actually hit our payment provider's API endpoint over HTTP, we would get a lot of declined transactions (assuming we are not storing and using real credit card numbers), which could lead to our account being suspended due to suspicions of fraud, putting our e-commerce application out of service. Also, if we were running a **continuous integration (CI)** server such as Jenkins, which did not have access to the public Internet, we would get failures in our CI builds due to failing tests that attempted to access the Internet.

There are a few approaches to solving this problem. In our tests, we attempted to mock our HTTP requests, but obviously failed to do so effectively. A second approach is to allow actual HTTP requests but to configure a special server for testing purposes. We'll discuss the second approach in more detail in *Chapter 5, Simulating External Services*. For now, let's focus on figuring out why our HTTP mocks were not successful. In a small set of tests like in this example, it is not hard to hunt down the places where we are sending actual HTTP requests. In larger code bases with a lot of test support code, it may be harder. Also, it would be nice to prevent access to the Internet altogether so we notice these issues as soon as we run the offending tests.

Fortunately, Ruby has many excellent tools for testing, and there is one that addresses our needs exactly: WebMock (`https://github.com/bblimke/webmock`). We simply install the gem and add a couple of lines to our spec helper file to disable all network connections in our tests:

```ruby
require 'rspec'

# require the webmock gem
require 'webmock/rspec'

RSpec.configure do |config|
  # this is done by default, but let's make it clear
  WebMock.disable_net_connect!

  Config.order            = 'random'
  config.profile_examples = 1
  config.color            = true
end
```

When we run our tests again, we'll see one or more instances of `WebMock::NetConne ctNotAllowedError`, along with a backtrace to lead us to the point in our tests where the HTTP request was made:

```
 2) OldWeatherQuery caching uses cached result in subsequent queries
    Failure/Error: weather_query.forecast('Malibu,US')
    WebMock::NetConnectNotAllowedError:
      Real HTTP connections are disabled. Unregistered request: GET http://api.
openweathermap.org/data/2.5/weather?q=Malibu,US with headers {'Accept'=>'*/*', '
Accept-Encoding'=>'gzip;q=1.0,deflate;q=0.6,identity;q=0.3', 'Host'=>'api.openwe
athermap.org', 'User-Agent'=>'Ruby'}

      You can stub this request with the following snippet:

      stub_request(:get, "http://api.openweathermap.org/data/2.5/weather?q=Mali
bu,US").
         with(:headers => {'Accept'=>'*/*', 'Accept-Encoding'=>'gzip;q=1.0,defla
te;q=0.6,identity;q=0.3', 'Host'=>'api.openweathermap.org', 'User-Agent'=>'Ruby'
}).
         to_return(:status => 200, :body => "", :headers => {})
```

If we examine our test code, we'll notice that we mock the `OldWeatherQuery.http` method in a few places. However, we forgot to set up the mock in the first `describe` block for caching where we defined a `json_response` object, but never mocked the `OldWeatherQuery.http` method to return `json_response`. We can solve the problem by mocking `OldWeatherQuery.http` throughout the entire test file. We'll also take this opportunity to clean up the initialization of `@api_request_count` in our code. Here's what we have now:

```ruby
# new_weather_query.rb

require 'net/http'
require 'json'
require 'timeout'

module NewWeatherQuery
  extend self

  class NetworkError < StandardError
  end

  def forecast(place, use_cache=true)
    add_to_history(place)
```

```
    if use_cache
      cache[place] ||= begin
        increment_api_request_count
        JSON.parse( http(place) )
      end
    else
      JSON.parse( http(place) )
    end
rescue JSON::ParserError => e
  raise NetworkError.new("Bad response: #{e.inspect}")
end

def increment_api_request_count
  @api_request_count ||= 0
  @api_request_count += 1
end

def api_request_count
  @api_request_count ||= 0
end

def history
  (@history || []).dup
end

def clear!
  @history           = []
  @cache             = {}
  @api_request_count = 0
end

private

def add_to_history(s)
  @history ||= []
  @history << s
end

def cache
  @cache ||= {}
end

BASE_URI = 'http://api.openweathermap.org/data/2.5/weather?q='
def http(place)
```

```
    uri = URI(BASE_URI + place)

    Net::HTTP.get(uri)
  rescue Timeout::Error
    raise NetworkError.new("Request timed out")
  rescue URI::InvalidURIError
    raise NetworkError.new("Bad place name: #{place}")
  rescue SocketError
    raise NetworkError.new("Could not reach #{uri.to_s}")
  end
end
```

And here is the spec file to go with it:

```
# spec/new_weather_query_spec.rb

require_relative 'spec_helper'
require_relative '../new_weather_query'

describe NewWeatherQuery do
  subject(:weather_query) { described_class }

  after { weather_query.clear! }

  let(:json_response) { '{}' }
  before do
    allow(weather_query).to receive(:http).and_return(json_response)
  end

  describe 'api_request is initialized' do
    it "does not raise an error" do
      weather_query.forecast('Malibu,US')
    end
  end

  describe 'caching' do
    let(:json_response) do
      '{"weather" : { "description" : "Sky is Clear"}}'
    end

    around(:example) do |example|
      actual = weather_query.send(:cache)
      expect(actual).to eq({})

      example.run
```

```
      end

      it "stores results in local cache" do
        weather_query.forecast('Malibu,US')

        actual = weather_query.send(:cache)
        expect(actual.keys).to eq(['Malibu,US'])
        expect(actual['Malibu,US']).to be_a(Hash)
      end

      it "uses cached result in subsequent queries" do
        weather_query.forecast('Malibu,US')
        weather_query.forecast('Malibu,US')
        weather_query.forecast('Malibu,US')
      end
    end

    describe 'query history' do
      before do
        expect(weather_query.history).to eq([])
      end

      it "stores every place requested" do
        places = %w(
          Malibu,US
          Beijing,CN
          Delhi,IN
          Malibu,US
          Malibu,US
          Beijing,CN
        )

        places.each {|s| weather_query.forecast(s) }

        expect(weather_query.history).to eq(places)
      end

      it "does not allow history to be modified" do
        expect {
          weather_query.history = ['Malibu,CN']
        }.to raise_error

        weather_query.history << 'Malibu,CN'
        expect(weather_query.history).to eq([])
```

```
      end
  end

  describe 'number of API requests' do
    before do
      expect(weather_query.api_request_count).to eq(0)
    end

    it "stores every place requested" do
      places = %w(
        Malibu,US
        Beijing,CN
        Delhi,IN
        Malibu,US
        Malibu,US
        Beijing,CN
      )

      places.each {|s| weather_query.forecast(s) }

      expect(weather_query.api_request_count).to eq(3)
    end

    it "does not allow count to be modified" do
      expect {
        weather_query.api_request_count = 100
      }.to raise_error

      expect {
        weather_query.api_request_count += 10
      }.to raise_error

      expect(weather_query.api_request_count).to eq(0)
    end
  end
end
```

Now we've fixed a major bug with our code that slipped through our specs and used to pass randomly. We've made it so that our tests always pass, regardless of the order in which they are run, and without needing to access the Internet. Our test code and application code has also become clearer as we've reduced duplication in a few places.

A case study of production faithfulness with a test resource instance

We're not done with our `WeatherQuery` example just yet. Let's take a look at how we would add a simple database to store our cached values. There are some serious limitations to the way we are caching with instance variables, which persist only within the scope of a single Ruby process. As soon as we stop or restart our app, the entire cache will be lost. In a production app, we would likely have many processes running the same code in order to serve traffic effectively. With our current approach, each process would have a separate cache, which would be very inefficient. We could easily save many HTTP requests if we were able to share the cache between processes and across restarts. Economizing on these requests is not simply a matter of improved response time. We also need to consider that we cannot make unlimited requests to external services. For commercial services, we would pay for the number of requests we make. For free services, we are likely to get throttled if we exceed some threshold. Therefore, an effective caching scheme that reduces the number of HTTP requests we make to our external services is of vital importance to the function of a real-world app. Finally, our cache is very simplistic and has no expiration mechanism short of clearing all entries. For a cache to be effective, we need to be able to store entries for individual locations for some period of time within which we don't expect the weather forecast to change much. This will keep the cache small and up to date.

We'll use Redis (`http://redis.io`) as our database since it is very fast, simple, and easy to set up. You can find instructions on the Redis website on how to install it, which is an easy process on any platform. Once you have Redis installed, you simply need to start the server locally, which you can do with the `redis-server` command. We'll also need to install the Redis Ruby client as a gem (`https://github.com/redis/redis-rb`).

Let's start with a separate configuration file to set up our Redis client for our tests:

```ruby
# spec/config/redis.rb

require 'rspec'
require 'redis'

ENV['WQ_REDIS_URL'] ||= 'redis://localhost:6379/15'

RSpec.configure do |config|
  if ! ENV['WQ_REDIS_URL'].is_a?(String)
    raise "WQ_REDIS_URL environment variable not set"
  end
```

```
    ::REDIS_CLIENT = Redis.new( :url => ENV['WQ_REDIS_URL'] )

    config.after(:example, :redis) do
      ::REDIS_CLIENT.flushdb
    end
  end
end
```

Note that we place this file in a new `config` folder under our main `spec` folder. The idea is to configure each resource separately in its own file to keep everything isolated and easy to understand. This will make maintenance easy and prevent problems with configuration management down the road.

We don't do much in this file, but we do establish some important conventions. There is a single environment variable, which takes care of the Redis connection URL. By using an environment variable, we make it easy to change configuration and also allow flexibility in how these configurations are stored. Our code doesn't care if the Redis connection URL is stored in a simple `.env` file with key-value pairs or loaded from a configuration database. We can also easily override this value manually simply by setting it when we run RSpec, like so:

```
$ WQ_REDIS_URL=redis://1.2.3.4:4321/0 rspec spec
```

Note that we also set a sensible default value, which is to run on the default Redis port of 6379 on our local machine, on database number 15, which is less likely to be used for local development. This prevents our tests from relying on our development database, or from polluting or destroying it. It is also worth mentioning that we prefix our environment variable with **WQ** (short for **weather query**). Small details like this are very important for keeping our code easy to understand and to prevent dangerous clashes. We could imagine the kinds of confusion and clashes that could be caused if we relied on `REDIS_URL` and we had multiple apps running on the same server, all relying on Redis. It would be very easy to break many applications if we changed the value of `REDIS_URL` for a single app to point to a different instance of Redis. (We'll explore configuration in much greater depth in *Chapter 9, Configurability*.)

We set a global constant, `::REDIS_CLIENT`, to point to a Redis client. We will use this in our code to connect to Redis. Note that in real-world code, we would likely have a global namespace for the entire app and we would define globals such as `REDIS_CLIENT` under that namespace rather than in the global Ruby namespace.

Finally, we configure RSpec to call the `flushdb` command after every example tagged with `:redis` to empty the database and keep state clean across tests. In our code, all tests interact with Redis, so this tag seems pointless. However, it is very likely that we would add code that had nothing to do with Redis, and using tags helps us to constrain the scope of our configuration hooks only to where they are needed. This will also prevent confusion about multiple hooks running for the same example. In general, we want to prevent global hooks where possible and make configuration hooks explicitly triggered where possible.

So what does our spec look like now? Actually, it is almost exactly the same. Only a few lines have changed to work with the new Redis cache. See if you can spot them!

```ruby
# spec/redis_weather_query_spec.rb

require_relative 'spec_helper'
require_relative '../redis_weather_query'

describe RedisWeatherQuery, redis: true do
  subject(:weather_query) { described_class }

  after { weather_query.clear! }

  let(:json_response) { '{}' }
  before do
    allow(weather_query).to receive(:http).and_return(json_response)
  end

  describe 'api_request is initialized' do
    it "does not raise an error" do
      weather_query.forecast('Malibu,US')
    end
  end

    describe 'caching' do
    let(:json_response) do
      '{"weather" : { "description" : "Sky is Clear"}}'
    end

    around(:example) do |example|
      actual = weather_query.send(:cache).all
      expect(actual).to eq({})

      example.run
    end
```

```ruby
    it "stores results in local cache" do
      weather_query.forecast('Malibu,US')

      actual = weather_query.send(:cache).all
      expect(actual.keys).to eq(['Malibu,US'])
      expect(actual['Malibu,US']).to be_a(Hash)
    end

    it "uses cached result in subsequent queries" do
      weather_query.forecast('Malibu,US')
      weather_query.forecast('Malibu,US')
      weather_query.forecast('Malibu,US')
    end
  end

  describe 'query history' do
    before do
      expect(weather_query.history).to eq([])
    end

    it "stores every place requested" do
      places = %w(
        Malibu,US
        Beijing,CN
        Delhi,IN
        Malibu,US
        Malibu,US
        Beijing,CN
      )

      places.each {|s| weather_query.forecast(s) }

      expect(weather_query.history).to eq(places)
    end

    it "does not allow history to be modified" do
      expect {
        weather_query.history = ['Malibu,CN']
      }.to raise_error

      weather_query.history << 'Malibu,CN'
      expect(weather_query.history).to eq([])
    end
  end
```

```
describe 'number of API requests' do
  before do
    expect(weather_query.api_request_count).to eq(0)
  end

  it "stores every place requested" do
    places = %w(
      Malibu,US
      Beijing,CN
      Delhi,IN
      Malibu,US
      Malibu,US
      Beijing,CN
    )

    places.each {|s| weather_query.forecast(s) }

    expect(weather_query.api_request_count).to eq(3)
  end

  it "does not allow count to be modified" do
    expect {
      weather_query.api_request_count = 100
    }.to raise_error

    expect {
      weather_query.api_request_count += 10
    }.to raise_error

    expect(weather_query.api_request_count).to eq(0)
  end
end
end
```

So what about the actual WeatherQuery code? It changes very little as well:

```
# redis_weather_query.rb

require 'net/http'
require 'json'
require 'timeout'

# require the new cache module
require_relative 'redis_weather_cache'
```

```ruby
module RedisWeatherQuery
  extend self

  class NetworkError < StandardError
  end

  # ... same as before ...

  def clear!
    @history           = []
    @api_request_count = 0

    # no more clearing of cache here
  end

  private

  # ... same as before ...

  # the new cache module has a Hash-like interface
  def cache
    RedisWeatherCache
  end

  # ... same as before ...

end
```

We can see that we've preserved pretty much the same code and specs as before. Almost all of the new functionality is accomplished in a new module that caches with Redis. Here is what it looks like:

```ruby
# redis_weather_cache.rb

require 'redis'

module RedisWeatherCache
  extend self

  CACHE_KEY             = 'weather_query:cache'
  EXPIRY_ZSET_KEY       = 'weather_query:expiry_tracker'
  EXPIRE_FORECAST_AFTER = 300 # 5 minutes

  def redis_client
    if ! defined?(::REDIS_CLIENT)
```

```ruby
      raise("No REDIS_CLIENT defined!")
    end

    ::REDIS_CLIENT
  end

  def []=(location, forecast)
    redis_client.hset(CACHE_KEY, location, JSON.generate(forecast))
    redis_client.zadd(EXPIRY_ZSET_KEY, Time.now.to_i, location)
  end

  def [](location)
    remove_expired_entries

    raw_value = redis_client.hget(CACHE_KEY, location)

    if raw_value
      JSON.parse(raw_value)
    else
      nil
    end
  end

  def all
    redis_client.hgetall(CACHE_KEY).inject({}) do |memo, (location,
forecast_json)|
      memo[location] = JSON.parse(forecast_json)
      memo
    end
  end

  def clear!
    redis_client.del(CACHE_KEY)
  end

  def remove_expired_entries
    # expired locations have a score, i.e. creation timestamp, less
than a certain threshold
    expired_locations = redis_client.zrangebyscore(EXPIRY_ZSET_KEY, 0,
Time.now.to_i - EXPIRE_FORECAST_AFTER)

    if ! expired_locations.empty?
      # remove the cache entry
      redis_client.hdel(CACHE_KEY, expired_locations)
```

```
        # also clear the expiry entry
        redis_client.zrem(EXPIRY_ZSET_KEY, expired_locations)
      end
    end
  end
```

We'll avoid a detailed explanation of this code. We simply note that we accomplish all of the design goals we discussed at the beginning of the section: a persistent cache with expiration of individual values. We've accomplished this using some simple Redis functionality along with ZSET or sorted set functionality, which is a bit more complex, and which we needed because Redis does not allow individual entries in a Hash to be deleted. We can see that by using method names such as RedisWeatherCache.[] and RedisWeatherCache.[]=, we've maintained a Hash-like interface, which made it easy to use this cache instead of the simple in-memory Ruby Hash we had in our previous iteration. Our tests all pass and are still pretty simple, thanks to the modularity of this new cache code, the modular configuration file, and the previous fixes we made to our specs to remove Internet and run-order dependencies.

Summary

In this chapter, we delved into setting up and cleaning up state for real-world specs that interact with external services and local resources by extending our WeatherQuery example to address a big bug, isolate our specs from the Internet, and cleanly configure a Redis database to serve as a better cache.

In the following chapter, we'll learn more advanced examples of managing external service dependencies using smarter mocks and the VCR gem.

5
Simulating External Services

In *Chapter 4*, *Setting Up and Cleaning Up*, we learned how to manage external resources such as databases and web services. In this chapter, we'll learn more advanced techniques for managing external web services using the VCR gem, which allows us to record real HTTP requests and then replay them in our tests.

The importance of external web services

It is increasingly common for software to rely on external web services. These can be from a third party, such as the openweathermap.org API we saw in *Chapter 4*, *Setting Up and Cleaning Up*. However, we are likely to also interact with web services from within our own organization, or those that we have written ourselves. Not only do web services allow us to access external tools, such as weather info from openweathermap.org, they are also a popular approach to architecting applications within an organization. It is safe to say that an HTTP API is the default approach to exposing a service over a network today.

Dealing with external web services in tests can be challenging. By definition, these services are external, so we don't have as much, or any, control over how they behave, or how much support they offer for testing. As we saw in *Chapter 4*, *Setting Up and Cleaning Up*, we should try to avoid these external services in most tests, so we need to mock them. These mocks need to be realistic but also simple enough to manage. This is a fundamental trade-off, as the more realistic the mocks are, the closer they are to the actual service being mocked, requiring much more complexity.

For example, if we wanted to mock the OpenWeatherMap web service for just a few requests to return the same data every time, our mocks would be simple. However, there are countless requests that we could make to OpenWeatherMap for countless places all over the world. And, of course, the weather is always changing, so the same request would return different results at different times. Finally, there may be intermittent unexpected responses to certain requests, for example, when the service is down, or if there is an unexpected error retrieving weather data for a particular location. If we tried to deal with each of these situations in our mock service, we would soon have a lot of complex code that's just for tests. The bad thing about this is that our tests would be harder to understand, and the likelihood of mistakes in the mock code would increase. The testability of our system would not be improved in such a scenario unless we devoted a large amount of time to developing and maintaining the mocks.

In certain cases, such an intensive effort is justified, but most of the time, we would be better served by leveraging the real external web service. The idea is simple. We send a number of real requests to the external service, and record the responses along with the requests. In our tests, we can simply mock the response for a request by looking it up in our recordings. In case we don't find any recorded response for a request in our tests, we can either raise an error, or send a request to the real external service. If we wanted to make things very easy to maintain, we could have a script that updated all of our recordings on demand, allowing us to keep up with any changes to the responses of the external service. This way we would detect issues such as changed response formats and deprecated API endpoints.

Mock HTTP responses with custom helpers

In the specs for the RedisWeatherQuery module that we worked with in *Chapter 4, Setting Up and Cleaning Up*, we mocked HTTP responses to prevent actual requests being sent during test runs. The code that accomplished this was simple:

```
let(:json_response) { '{}' }

before do
  allow(weather_query).to receive(:http).and_return(json_response)
end
```

For most specs, we actually don't need any mock response data, so an empty `Hash` is good enough. But this approach has some problems. First, we may want to validate the response we receive from the API to ensure it meets our expectations of how it is formatted. Second, we may have mocks in our specs that do not look like anything that the API returns. Third, we are treating the response imprecisely, ignoring the HTTP status code, assuming the body is valid JSON, and caching all responses regardless of success or failure status.

All these shortcomings will lead to bugs in our real-world code. Also, debugging will be difficult since we do not clearly isolate issues with the API response from issues with our own code. In order to improve our tests and code, we need to look closer at real-world responses from the external service we are using.

Using real-world requests for mock responses

Let's address some of the problems we identified with our simplistic mock responses. We'll send a few real requests to the `OpenWeatherMap` API and adjust our mocks based on the real responses we get.

First, let's set up a little script to help us make requests:

```ruby
#!/usr/bin/env ruby

require_relative 'redis_weather_query'
require 'json'

REDIS_CLIENT = Redis.new

if ARGV.size != 1
  abort "usage: #{__FILE__} <location>"
end

location  = ARGV.shift
response  = RedisWeatherQuery.forecast(location)
formatted = JSON.pretty_generate(response)

puts formatted

exit 0
```

Let's put this file in the same folder as `redis_weather_query.rb` and `redis_weather_cache.rb`, then use it to make a few requests. We'll name the file `rwb.rb` and make sure it is executable.

Here is what we get for a successful search for `half moon bay`:

```
● ● ●                          Terminal
$ ./rwb.rb half moon bay
{
  "coord": {
    "lon": -122.43,
    "lat": 37.46
  },
  "weather": [
    {
      "id": 701,
      "main": "Mist",
      "description": "mist",
      "icon": "50n"
    }
  ],
  "base": "cmc stations",
  "main": {
    "temp": 291.22,
    "pressure": 1015,
    "humidity": 88,
    "temp_min": 288.15,
    "temp_max": 293.75
  },
  "wind": {
    "speed": 5.7,
    "deg": 320,
    "gust": 8.7
  },
  "clouds": {
    "all": 90
  },
  "dt": 1436851766,
  "sys": {
    "type": 1,
    "id": 392,
    "message": 0.0072,
    "country": "US",
    "sunrise": 1436878803,
    "sunset": 1436931050
  },
  "id": 5354943,
  "name": "Half Moon Bay",
  "cod": 200
}
$
```

So far, so good. Let's see what happens when the search is not successful:

```
● ● ●                          Terminal
$ ./rwb.rb AJKDFH
{
  "cod": "404",
  "message": "Error: Not found city"
}
$ ./rwb.rb 北京
/Users/mani/repos/rspec-essentials/book/05/01-improved-error-handling/redis_weat
her_query.rb:68:in `rescue in http': Bad place name: 北京 (RedisWeatherQuery::Ne
tworkError)
        from /Users/mani/repos/rspec-essentials/book/05/01-improved-error-handli
ng/redis_weather_query.rb:62:in `http'
        from /Users/mani/repos/rspec-essentials/book/05/01-improved-error-handli
ng/redis_weather_query.rb:19:in `forecast'
        from ./rwb.rb:13:in `<main>'
$ ./rwb.rb Москва
/Users/mani/repos/rspec-essentials/book/05/01-improved-error-handling/redis_weat
her_query.rb:68:in `rescue in http': Bad place name: Москва (RedisWeatherQuery::
NetworkError)
        from /Users/mani/repos/rspec-essentials/book/05/01-improved-error-handli
ng/redis_weather_query.rb:62:in `http'
        from /Users/mani/repos/rspec-essentials/book/05/01-improved-error-handli
ng/redis_weather_query.rb:19:in `forecast'
        from ./rwb.rb:13:in `<main>'
$ █
```

In the first case, we passed a nonsense place name, and the response looks good. Maybe we would rather return `nil` or raise an error, but the current behavior is also not bad.

The second and third examples are problems. We may wonder if the `OpenWeatherMap` API can handle non-ASCII characters in its searches. We can try to access the API in a browser or via `curl` to confirm that `OpenWeatherMap` does in fact handle such characters properly:

```
● ● ●                            Terminal
$ curl 'http://api.openweathermap.org/data/2.5/weather?q=北京'
{"coord":{"lon":116.4,"lat":39.91},"weather":[{"id":800,"main":"Clear","descript
ion":"Sky is Clear","icon":"01d"}],"base":"cmc stations","main":{"temp":307.71,"
pressure":1003,"humidity":30,"temp_min":303.15,"temp_max":312.04},"wind":{"speed
":4,"deg":170},"clouds":{"all":0},"dt":1436852112,"sys":{"type":1,"id":7405,"mes
sage":0.0119,"country":"CN","sunrise":1436821038,"sunset":1436874166},"id":18166
70,"name":"Beijing","cod":200}
$ curl 'http://api.openweathermap.org/data/2.5/weather?q=Москва'
{"coord":{"lon":37.62,"lat":55.75},"weather":[{"id":802,"main":"Clouds","descrip
tion":"scattered clouds","icon":"03d"}],"base":"cmc stations","main":{"temp":286
.96,"pressure":1007,"humidity":71,"temp_min":286.15,"temp_max":287.95},"wind":{"
speed":2},"clouds":{"all":40},"dt":1436852112,"sys":{"type":1,"id":7323,"message
":0.0121,"country":"RU","sunrise":1436835854,"sunset":1436897135},"id":524901,"n
ame":"Moscow","cod":200}
$ ▮
```

So the problem is with our code, not the API. Let's take these real requests and responses and update our specs with them. We'll create a new spec file for **end-to-end (e2e)** tests. To mimic real responses, we'll create a separate file for each request with a folder called `http_requests` inside the `spec` folder. Each file's name is the place name for the request and the file contains the raw response body we got from the API in our real-world requests. We'll still avoid making any real HTTP requests, but instead of responding with an empty JSON object, as in our last version of the specs, we'll use the files in `http_requests` to mock the response of `Net::HTTP.get` to simulate what we would get from the real API:

```
require 'uri'
require 'json'
require_relative 'spec_helper'
require_relative '../redis_weather_query'

describe RedisWeatherQuery, redis: true do
  subject(:weather_query) { described_class }

  after { weather_query.clear! }

  context 'end-to-end tests based on real requests' do
    http_requests = begin
```

```
    here          = File.dirname(__FILE__)
    glob_pattern  = here + '/http_requests/*'

    Dir[glob_pattern].inject({}) do |memo, path|
      place_name = File.basename(path)
      response   = File.read(path)

      memo[place_name] = response
      memo
    end
  end

  before(:example) do
    allow(Net::HTTP).to receive(:get) do |uri_object|
      query = uri_object.query
      place = URI.decode( query.split('=').last )

      http_requests[ place.force_encoding('utf-8') ]
    end
  end

  http_requests.each do |place, raw_response|
    it "returns the expected response for #{place}" do
      actual    = weather_query.forecast(place)
      expected  = JSON.parse(raw_response)

      expect(actual).to eq(expected)
    end
  end
 end
end
```

There are two new tricks in these specs that we should go over.

First, we use the block form of `allow` to set up our mock HTTP responses. This allows us to dynamically define mocks for multiple requests. The block variable `uri_object` is what `Net::HTTP.get` receives and the return value of the block is what will be used as the return value. We are basically intercepting HTTP requests and using the text stored in our text files as the response body.

Second, we are declaring `it` blocks inside a loop. This is not a good idea in general since we can easily get confused about what our specs are actually doing. Also, error messages can be more difficult to pin down, since it will be harder to track down which test case failed and we won't be able to easily run a single test case by specifying a line number for the spec. In some cases, however, declaring specs in this way can be very helpful. In our usage, we can simply add more files to the `http_requests` folder without having to change any code. Our specs are very simple and the place name is included in the spec name (the string following it) so this is one of the rare cases where it is helpful to declare specs in this way.

Let's see what happens when we run our specs:

```
● ● ●                              Terminal
$ rspec spec/redis_weather_query_e2e_spec.rb
..FF

Failures:

  1) RedisWeatherQuery end-to-end tests based on real requests returns the expec
ted response for Москва
     Failure/Error: actual    = weather_query.forecast(place)
     RedisWeatherQuery::NetworkError:
       Bad place name: Москва
     # ./redis_weather_query.rb:68:in `rescue in http'
     # ./redis_weather_query.rb:62:in `http'
     # ./redis_weather_query.rb:19:in `forecast'
     # ./spec/redis_weather_query_e2e_spec.rb:37:in `block (4 levels) in <top (r
equired)>'

  2) RedisWeatherQuery end-to-end tests based on real requests returns the expec
ted response for 北京
     Failure/Error: actual    = weather_query.forecast(place)
     RedisWeatherQuery::NetworkError:
       Bad place name: 北京
     # ./redis_weather_query.rb:68:in `rescue in http'
     # ./redis_weather_query.rb:62:in `http'
     # ./redis_weather_query.rb:19:in `forecast'
     # ./spec/redis_weather_query_e2e_spec.rb:37:in `block (4 levels) in <top (r
equired)>'

Finished in 0.01248 seconds (files took 0.29182 seconds to load)
4 examples, 2 failures

Failed examples:

rspec ./spec/redis_weather_query_e2e_spec.rb:36 # RedisWeatherQuery end-to-end t
ests based on real requests returns the expected response for Москва
rspec ./spec/redis_weather_query_e2e_spec.rb:36 # RedisWeatherQuery end-to-end t
ests based on real requests returns the expected response for 北京

$
```

Our tests now replicate the bug with our code that we encountered when running `rwb.rb` manually and hitting the real API. If we look into our code for `RedisWeatherQuery`, we can see that the error message generated in both cases is used when there is `URI::InvalidURIError`, which we rescue before raising a custom `RedisWeatherQuery:: NetworkError` exception. The problem is actually with our request and not the response (which actually never gets sent since the URI is not sent). The code that forms the URL that we use for the request is too naïve:

```
BASE_URI = 'http://api.openweathermap.org/data/2.5/weather?q='
def http(place)
  uri = URI(BASE_URI + place)
  # ...
end
```

Simply adding place to `BASE_URI` like this obviously does not handle non-ASCII strings properly. As RFC 2396 (`https://www.ietf.org/rfc/rfc2396.txt`) and the updated RFC 3986 (`https://tools.ietf.org/html/rfc3986`) state, characters in a URI must be encoded in US ASCII. For characters that cannot be represented by ASCII, percent encoding must be used.

To fix this bug, all we need to do is to use `URI.escape` on our URI before we pass it to `URI()`. So, our code should now look like this:

```
def http(place)
  uri = URI( URI.escape(BASE_URI + place) )
  # ...
end
```

If we run our specs now, they will all pass. We can also run `rwb.rb` and it will no longer raise an error for non-ASCII place names.

Using WebMock for mock HTTP requests

We didn't actually need to set up our own custom HTTP request mocks. We could have used `WebMock` to do it for us. Of course, it is always good to understand how to do things on our own before jumping straight into an external library. `WebMock` offers a few advantages. We can more easily match requests according to various criteria based on HTTP headers, method, and body. Also, `WebMock` works with a number of different HTTP libraries, so we could use the same mock code even if we chose to use an alternative to `Net::HTTP`. All we have to do is to change our `before(:example)` block in our spec like so:

```
before(:example) do
  WebMock.stub_request(:get, /api\.openweathermap\.org.+/).to_return
do |request|
```

```
    place    = URI.decode( request.uri.query.split('=').last )
    response = http_requests[ place.force_encoding('utf-8') ]

    { :body => response }
  end
end
```

We are using a regular expression to match all GET requests to api.weathermap.
org and specifying a body based on our files in the http_requests folder, just like
before. This is interesting, but what do we do when we want to update our mock
HTTP responses or add new ones? It's important to check our mocks against real
requests from time to time, as APIs do change. Right now, the process is completely
manual. We could write some helper scripts to help us with this task. Perhaps we
would like something more sophisticated that would allow us to specify the request
HTTP method and headers to match. We may also want to specify more about the
responses, including headers and status code. Luckily for us, the VCR gem does all
of this and more.

Using VCR for mock requests

VCR is a popular tool for recording and replaying HTTP requests. VCR was created
by Myron Marston, who also happens to be the lead developer of RSpec. Although
it is much more sophisticated than our primitive HTTP request mocking setup,
at its heart, VCR works the same way: it records real HTTP requests to files and
replays them during specs. The nice thing about VCR is that it does everything in a
configurable and automated way. We can tap into recorded HTTP requests with a
small configuration file and an RSpec tag, so we don't actually have much code in
our specs related to mocking HTTP requests. We can also record new HTTP requests
very easily to a new cassette (the term used by VCR for the file that records the HTTP
request and response) or to update an existing cassette. Finally, we can easily turn
our end-to-end tests into integration tests that actually hit real HTTP endpoints. In
short, VCR gives us many more options and simplifies our test code.

Let's see how it works with a realistic but minimal configuration. First, we'll modify
our spec_helper.rb file to load a new configuration file for VCR. We'll also allow
real network connections to be enabled using an environment variable:

```
require 'rspec'
require 'webmock/rspec'

require_relative 'config/redis'
require_relative 'config/vcr'
```

```
RSpec.configure do |config|
  if ENV['ALLOW_NET_CONNECT']
    WebMock.allow_net_connect!
  else
    WebMock.disable_net_connect!
  end

  config.order           = 'random'
  config.profile_examples = 1
  config.color           = true
end
```

Here's what we have in `config/vcr.rb`:

```
if ENV['ALLOW_NET_CONNECT']
  VCR_RECORD_MODE='irrelevant'
else
  require 'vcr'

  VCR_RECORD_MODE = (ENV['VCR_RECORD_MODE'] || :none).to_sym

  VCR.configure do |c|
    c.cassette_library_dir = 'spec/cassettes'
    c.hook_into :webmock
    c.configure_rspec_metadata!
  end
end
```

Note that `VCR` integrates with `WebMock` and, with our setup, we can bypass both to hit the real `OpenWeatherMap` API by setting the `ALLOW_NET_CONNECT` environment variable when running `RSpec`. Also note that when we set `ALLOW_NET_CONNECT`, we don't even require the `VCR` gem, so it should have no effect during our test run. We have another environment variable, `VCR_RECORD_MODE`, which controls whether `VCR` records any HTTP interactions, and if so, which ones. By default, we don't record any HTTP requests. This helps to keep our tests deterministic, forcing us to explicitly record new HTTP requests by setting `VCR_RECORD_MODE` to once or all.

Next, we tell `VCR` where to store its cassettes, to use `WebMock`, and to activate `RSpec` metadata support, which will allow us to enable `VCR` and set options just by tagging our `RSpec` examples using the `:vcr` tag.

Now, let's have a look at our spec:

```
require 'uri'
require 'json'
require_relative 'spec_helper'
require_relative '../redis_weather_query'

describe RedisWeatherQuery, :vcr => {:record => VCR_RECORD_MODE},
redis: true do
  subject(:weather_query) { described_class }

  after { weather_query.clear! }

  context 'end-to-end tests based on real requests' do
    let(:actual) { weather_query.forecast(place) }

    context 'half moon bay' do
      let(:place)  { 'half moon bay' }

      it 'returns a found response' do
        expect(actual).to be_a(Hash)
        expect(actual['cod']).to eq(200)
      end
    end

    context 'Moscow' do
      let(:place)  { 'Москва' }

      it 'returns a found response' do
        expect(actual).to be_a(Hash)
        expect(actual['cod']).to eq(200)
      end
    end

    context 'Beijing' do
      let(:place)  { '北京' }

      it 'returns a found response' do
        expect(actual).to be_a(Hash)
        expect(actual['cod']).to eq(200)
      end
    end

    context 'AJKDFH' do
```

```
      let(:place)   { 'AJKDFH' }

      it 'returns a found response' do
        expect(actual).to be_a(Hash)
        expect(actual['cod']).to eq('404')
      end
    end
  end
end
```

We can see that we are setting a tag on the first `describe` block to configure `VCR` with the `record` mode that we set in the `config` file. The actual specs look a lot simpler. We are only looking at the `cod` key in the JSON that the API returns. The reason for this is that once we start recording a bunch of HTTP requests, we notice that much of the info we receive changes on every request because the weather doesn't stay the same even for a moment. We can do more complex matching, but it doesn't really serve much purpose since we would be comparing the `VCR` recorded response against itself most of the time, and when we bypassed `VCR`, it would be likely that our specs would fail for no good reason. Keep in mind that errors in our code sending the request or processing the response would still be caught.

We also removed the looping to create multiple test cases. Since we don't have the same visibility into what is recorded, it is a good idea to make it clear what places we are searching for. Otherwise, we could wind up not knowing how many cassettes we have or for which locations. Worse, the cassettes could change over time, making our tests very unstable. This is also why we set the default record mode to `:none` so that we don't start recording all kinds of cassettes without even noticing.

Let's run our specs and see what happens:

```
$ rspec spec/redis_weather_query_e2e_vcr_spec.rb

Randomized with seed 53199
FFFF

Failures:

  1) RedisWeatherQuery end-to-end tests based on real requests Beijing returns a
  found response
     Failure/Error: let(:actual) { weather_query.forecast(place) }
     VCR::Errors::UnhandledHTTPRequestError:
```

I've only included the top part of the output, which is long, but we can see that all our specs fail with `VCR::Errors::UnhandledHTTPRequestError`. This is actually good, as we've confirmed that we won't hit the real API endpoint and record the request unless we set an environment variable. Let's do that and see what happens:

```
●  ●  ●                               Terminal
$ VCR_RECORD_MODE=once rspec spec/redis_weather_query_e2e_vcr_spec.rb

Randomized with seed 25505
. . . .

Top 1 slowest examples (0.27038 seconds, 27.8% of total time):
  RedisWeatherQuery end-to-end tests based on real requests half moon bay return
s a found response
    0.27038 seconds ./spec/redis_weather_query_e2e_vcr_spec.rb:17

Finished in 0.97394 seconds (files took 0.33372 seconds to load)
4 examples, 0 failures

Randomized with seed 25505

$ ▊
```

All our specs pass now. If you look inside the `spec` folder, you will see a folder called `cassettes`, inside of which, nested inside a few more folders, are a number of YAML files that record the HTTP response we got from the real API. If we run our specs one more time, without the environment variable, they will now all pass, since the cassettes are now there. We can also bypass VCR and WebMock by setting the `ALLOW_NET_CONNECT` environment variable, which will hit the real API endpoint but not update any cassettes.

There are many more options with VCR, but we can go very far with just these basics. The important thing is to understand how the basic mechanism works, to guard against excessive variability in our specs, and to decide when to record new cassettes.

Summary

In this chapter, we learned a few different ways of handling external web services in our tests, recording and replaying HTTP requests with our own custom code, WebMock, and, finally, VCR.

6

Driving a Web Browser with Capybara

In the preceding five chapters, we have covered all the important features of RSpec, focusing on unit tests for libraries and command-line tools. Now it is time to build on this foundation to learn how to write end-to-end tests for web applications. In order to test web applications in a realistic way, we need to a way to interact with a web browser in our tests. The **Capybara** gem allows us to control a variety of browsers from within our test code to interact with a web application and make assertions about the behavior of the application within the browser.

In this chapter, we'll get familiar with how Capybara works, and how it integrates with RSpec. Unlike the preceding chapters, in which we developed the application code alongside our test code, this time we are not going to build a new application but point our browser, via Capybara, to existing websites. This way, we can focus on understanding the test code. Nevertheless, don't worry, we will use our skills with Capybara and RSpec to build a web application from scratch in *Chapter 7, Building an App from the Outside in with Behavior-Driven Development*.

Here are the topics we'll learn about in this chapter:

- Features of Capybara and Selenium
- Controlling a browser with Capybara
- Using Capybara with RSpec
- Switching between Mozilla Firefox and Google Chrome in web app specs
- Using a headless driver for continuous integration servers
- The importance of black-box JavaScript tests for today's web apps

Getting started with Capybara and Selenium

We'll talk about why Capybara is useful and how we're going to use it in our tests in some depth. First, let's see how we can use it to control a browser to interact with a web page. We'll do this from `irb`, the Ruby console.

We'll need to install the Capybara and **Selenium/WebDriver** gems first:

```
$ gem install capybara selenium-webdriver
```

The above may take a couple of minutes, since there are a few dependencies for each gem. We'll also need to make sure Mozilla Firefox is installed on our system. Now we can go into `irb` and control Firefox with Ruby code!

```
Terminal
$ irb
irb(main):001:0> require 'capybara'
true
irb(main):002:0> Capybara.current_driver = :selenium
:selenium
irb(main):003:0> Capybara.visit 'http://si.edu'
""
irb(main):004:0>
```

We first require the Capybara gem, then we set the driver to use Selenium, since the default driver, `Rack::Test`, cannot control a real browser. Finally, we use the `Capybara.visit` method to browse to `http://si.edu`, the website for the Smithsonian Institution in Washington, DC. If all goes well, after you hit *Enter* for that last command, Firefox should launch and load the URL. You should see a page like the one below:

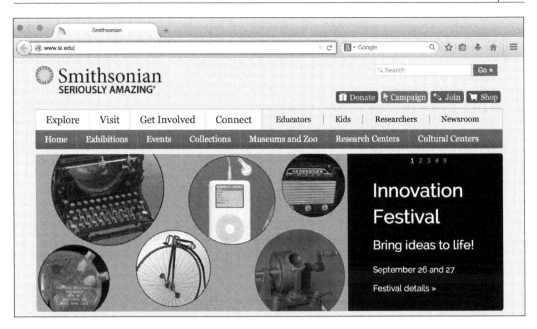

Now let's interact with the page. If you look in the top right, you'll see a **Search** form field. Let's use it to find some resources on the Wright brothers.

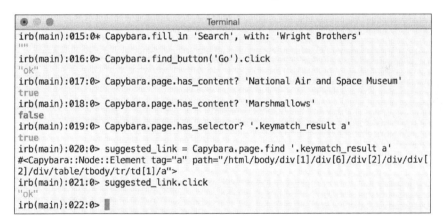

As you type in each command above, you should look at the Firefox browser to see how we first fill in the search term, click the **Go** button to load the search results, and then, finally, click on one of the links. You should see a page like this at the end of the process:

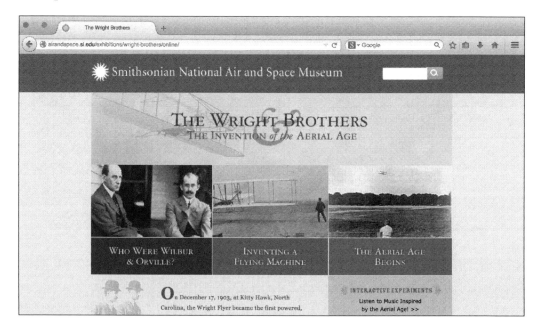

That's about it, actually. There are some important points about how to effectively configure and use Capybara and Selenium, but as for the actual features, we've covered all the important ones already:

- `Capybara.visit` to load a URL
- `Capybara.fill_in` to enter text into an input field
- `Capybara.find_button` to find a button element
- `Element.click` to click on an element (we'll also use `Capybara.click_on`)
- `Capybara.has_content?` to look for visible text on the page
- `Capybara.has_selector?` to look for a CSS selector on the page
- `Capybara.find` to retrieve an element on the page using a CSS selector

Now you should try out some things on your own in `irb` to get familiar with Capybara. Try to find some of the elements you see on the page. Finding elements by text can be tricky when there isn't a unique string, but you can use Firefox's Inspector to look at a page's HTML markup to find CSS selectors (`keymatch_result a` in the preceding example). You should also try to load other websites and see how Capybara handles more dynamic pages.

Integrating Capybara with RSpec

Let's turn our `irb` session into an RSpec spec to finish our initial tour of Capybara. We'll put the contents into a file called `smithsonian_spec.rb` that looks like this:

```
require 'capybara/rspec'

Capybara.current_driver = :selenium

# switch to chrome based on environment variable. e.g.:
#    $ BROWSER=chrome rspec smithsonian_spec.rb
if ENV['BROWSER'] == 'chrome'
  Capybara.register_driver :selenium do |app|
    Capybara::Selenium::Driver.new(app, browser: :chrome)
  end

# use poltergeist headless driver/browser based on environment
variable, e.g.
#    $ BROWSER=poltergeist rspec smithsonian_spec.rb
elseif ENV['BROWSER'] == 'poltergeist'
  puts "Using poltergeist headless driver..."

  require 'capybara/poltergeist'

  Capybara.register_driver :poltergeist do |app|
    Capybara::Poltergeist::Driver.new(app, {timeout: 60})
  end

  Capybara.current_driver = :poltergeist
end

describe "si.edu", type: :feature do
  it "has a search feature" do
    visit 'http://si.edu'

    fill_in "Search", :with => 'Wright Brothers'
```

```
    find_button('Go').click

    expect(page).to have_content('National Air and Space Museum')
    expect(page).to_not have_content('Marshmallows')

    expect(page).to have_selector('.keymatch_result a')

    suggested_link = page.find '.keymatch_result a'
    suggested_link.click

    expected_text = 'On December 17, 1903, at Kitty Hawk, North
Carolina, the Wright Flyer became the first powered, heavier-than-air
machine to achieve controlled, sustained flight with a pilot aboard.'

    expect(page).to have_content(expected_text)

    page.save_screenshot('wright-brothers.png')
  end
end
```

Now we'll run this like any other spec file:

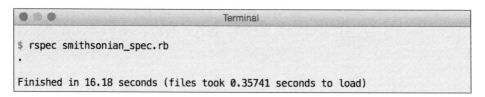

```
$ rspec smithsonian_spec.rb
.

Finished in 16.18 seconds (files took 0.35741 seconds to load)
```

When you run the rspec command, you will see Firefox open. Then it will start going through the actions defined in the spec file. There are a few new things here.

First, we see that there is a BROWSER environment variable that lets us switch to Google's Chrome browser. It's easy to try it out. You can install the chromedriver-helper gem and run the specs with the following command:

```
$ BROWSER=chrome rspec smithsonian_spec.rb
```

Chrome is quite a bit faster than Firefox, so it's not a bad idea to use it as the default browser in our web app integration tests.

We also note there is an option to use the **Poltergeist** headless driver. You can install the poltergeist gem and try this out with this command:

```
$ BROWSER=poltergeist rspec smithsonian_spec.rb
```

Don't worry if you don't see anything happening this time. That's the whole point. A headless browser interacts with web pages like a regular browser, but it's all done with no visible UI. This is very helpful for running browser tests as part of continuous integration tests on servers that do not have UIs or browsers installed.

Moving further down, we notice that we use the `:type => :feature` metadata to mark the spec as a `Capybara` spec. This makes the DSL methods available in our scope so we use `fill_in` instead of `Capybara.fill_in`.

Another thing worth noting is that we turn the query methods into assertions following the RSpec convention that a question method turns into a statement method (for example, `has_selector?` becomes `have_selector`).

Finally, we've taken a screenshot at the end of the spec. You should see the `wright-brothers.png` image file in the same folder as the spec file after you've run it. This screenshot feature is not only cool, but can help you document your web app. It's also helpful for debugging purposes. For example, you could automatically take a screenshot whenever a spec fails to help figure out the problem, since the spec failure message is often not enough info to pinpoint what went wrong.

Although we haven't written a lot of code, and we are all quite familiar with the browser, there is something magical about automatic browser interactions in tests. It still impresses me after years of working with them. One reason why is that we are actually taking control of our operating system using some rather advanced software in Selenium. Capybara hides the complexity from us, but we can feel its power as we watch the browser in action, as if under the influence of some "spooky action at a distance".

We've already learned some important facts about testing with Capybara.

First, we have to know something about the page structure we are working with. In order to find and interact with elements, we need either a unique bit of text or a specific CSS selector. This is a trade-off and often specs will start to fail due to small changes in labels or HTML structure.

Second, the tests are launching a real browser in our operating system. If we are running these tests on a server with no GUI, we'll have to figure out how we can install a working browser.

Third, the tests are pretty slow. If the site loaded faster, it would be a little better, but even the fastest pages will likely take 2 or 3 seconds per test. This means we have to limit the number of tests so that running them doesn't take forever.

Finally, our assertions are based on what is visible on the page. We could do something fancy, such as connect to a database to check for the result of an action we took, but that is unusual and goes against the concept of black-box testing, which we will discuss later. For now, we note that we also need to know something about the page structure and content to construct assertions.

Why Capybara?

Capybara's GitHub page describes it as an "acceptance test framework for web applications". We'll consider acceptance test to be a synonym for integration test or end-to-end test, although subtle distinctions can be made. Therefore, we already know that we won't be writing unit tests and that we will be dealing with a web application. Implicitly, this means we'll use a web browser. Capybara itself does not control the browser, but relies on drivers. The most popular of these is called Selenium, which is used widely for testing web applications. With Selenium, we can automate a real web browser, such as Mozilla Firefox, Google Chrome, Apple Safari, or Microsoft Edge, using code.

Why not just use Selenium directly? This is a good question. The Selenium team provides a gem called `selenium-webdriver`, which provides the basic browser control capabilities we need. However, Capybara has three major benefits, which explains why almost all web application test code in Ruby uses it (in fact, Capybara is so successful that even non-Ruby projects use it).

First, Capybara provides a simple, high-level, and smart interface for interacting with web applications. This allows for test code to clearly represent a realistic user flow in a very human-friendly syntax that looks like documentation of steps for a manual test. Further, the API avoids confusion and clutter from complex HTML and CSS fragments by allowing content to be found flexibly using text snippets. Capybara waits automatically for AJAX requests and JavaScript updates to the DOM, reducing annoying timing issues in tests. Selenium, on the other hand, provides a complex, low-level interface that is quite difficult to work with directly.

Second, there are good reasons to use other drivers besides Selenium. Headless drivers such as PhantomJS run tests much faster and are easier to install than Selenium, making them good choices for continuous integration servers that run end-to-end tests. Selenium itself has many configuration options that are easy to manage with Capybara. For example, it is often helpful to run the same set of tests on multiple browsers, and Capybara makes this very easy to accomplish.

Third, Capybara has a very rich set of helpers that address common testing needs. Querying for content can be done in many ways, ranging from complete precision to very loose scanning, to fit the needs of the particular situation. The same applies to interacting with elements on the page, or making assertions about it. For example, we can look for a specific CSS selector such as `#todo-items ul li.active` or just a snippet of text such as "current item". There are also nice features, such as the ability to take a screenshot anywhere in a running test.

We can still take advantage of advanced driver features because Capybara gives us direct access to the native underlying driver object. This is very important as certain basic actions, such as pressing *Enter* in an input field, or choosing an image to upload, can be quite difficult to do in automated tests. With Capybara's maturity and full feature set, we can be confident we won't run into test cases that we can't automate.

Capybara, like RSpec, is a very solid tool that has contributed to the excellence of testing in the Ruby community. I would be willing to wager that no other web application testing tool in any language can match up to Capybara. It actually makes sense in some cases to use Capybara to test web applications that are not even written in Ruby. We'll learn next about the black-box approach to testing, where we won't even concern ourselves with the language the web app is written in.

Black-box JavaScript tests with a real browser

Capybara's first gem release was in 2009. At that time, JavaScript was not required for many popular web pages, and a popular approach to web development was "unobtrusive JavaScript", which meant that the basic functionality of a web page was still available without JavaScript. The most popular framework for JavaScript was jQuery and single-page web app frameworks like Angular.js or React were not in wide use. In the intervening years, web pages have been steadily replaced by web apps, which require JavaScript for all functionality. The single-page web application is a very popular architecture and many frameworks exist to support it.

The reason for this history lesson is to put in context the choices we are going to make about how we use Capybara. The easiest way to use Capybara and the first thing documented in its README is to let Capybara start our web app automatically, allowing anything in the app to be mocked. To interact with the web app, a fake Ruby browser called `Rack::Test` is used. This "browser" ignores JavaScript completely and doesn't even make HTTP requests, as it interacts with the Ruby web server directly.

We won't spend any time going down this "easy" path since it no longer makes any sense. There is not much interest today in developing a web app in static HTML without JavaScript. To get JavaScript to run, we'll need a real browser of some kind. We'll start with Mozilla Firefox, which is the default for Selenium. Finally, we'll treat the HTTP API server as a black box, avoiding mocking. This will simplify our tests a great deal and keep us focused on end-to-end testing. There is room for mocking or lower-level tests using Capybara, but in the world of rich web apps, these use cases are now a niche, just like the static HTML website.

Summary

In this chapter, we delved into the basics of testing web apps using Capybara and Selenium. We learned how to control a browser, interact with a website, query its contents, and make assertions about it. We also learned about the importance of a black-box testing strategy to today's web apps, which rely on JavaScript for all functionality. In the next chapter, we will draw on what we learned here to build a web app of our own, starting with integration (or acceptance) tests, following a methodology known as BDD. Then, in *Chapter 8, Tackling the Challenges of End-to-end Testing*, we will learn about some challenges related to end-to-end testing of web apps and solve them by adjusting both our app code and our tests.

7
Building an App from the Outside In with Behavior-Driven Development

RSpec's home page describes it as:

Behaviour-Driven Development tool for Ruby programmers

– RSpec (https://www.relishapp.com/rspec)

In this chapter and the next one, we'll learn about **Behavior-Driven Development (BDD)** by building an app from the outside in, that is, by beginning with high-level acceptance tests that also serve as documentation for the important features of the app. We'll build the app from the outermost part (the user interface) inwards, through the controller portion, and, finally, to the model. We'll build on what we learned in the preceding chapter on automated browser testing with Capybara to create an executable feature file that defines our high-level behavior for our app.

Here are some of the things we'll learn in this chapter:

- BDD and its relation to testing
- Defining a **minimum marketable feature (MMF)**
- Building web apps with Rack

Exploring BDD

We have discussed testing and testability with a view to ensuring high-quality code. But what about the feature itself? What use are excellent code and tests if the feature itself is bad? Indeed, software engineers have struggled to find ways of improving the overall quality of the system they work on. One of the more successful, and more popular, methods of addressing the problem of feature or product quality in software is BDD, which was developed in the mid-2000s by Dan North, Martin Fowler, and Aslak Hellesoy. This methodology seeks to describe the behavior of software from the outside in and justify this behavior in terms of business value. BDD developed alongside RSpec, which was the first widely used BDD framework. Therefore, it is natural that we explore the methodology so that we understand the motivation behind RSpec itself.

BDD concerns itself with ensuring that the right software is developed. Contrast this with our typical concern when writing tests, which is to ensure that the software works in the right way. Usually, when we write a test, even if we write the test before the code, as in test-driven development, we don't spend much time thinking about why we think the particular feature is valuable or justified. In fact, if we are writing a unit test for an individual method, such considerations are not even meaningful. It is to be hoped that, at some point, thought was given to the usefulness and value of the overall feature, but usually this effort is excluded from our testing efforts, and the software development process as a whole, actually.

A simple way of understanding BDD is that it forces us to ask "why?" Why do we need a particular feature? Can it be removed? Which features do we really need and which are just nice to have?

Another aspect of BDD is that the specification should be written in plain English to encourage understanding and discussion while minimizing implementation details. Purists may choose to use the Cucumber framework instead of RSpec, but we can achieve the same goal with RSpec, which, like the Ruby programming language, favors a syntax that is close to natural English.

BDD is a rather strict and well-defined methodology. We'll describe its rules clearly here, but we won't be purist in the subsequent pages, as we are more concerned with adapting some of its ideas to real-world use with RSpec. At the end of this chapter, we'll discuss in greater depth why BDD purism is not generally doable.

According to BDD, the right software delivers MMFs that offer the most business value. Software features should map directly to business value and nothing else. What is business value? According to BDD, there are only six categories:

- Protect revenue
- Increase revenue
- Manage cost
- Increase brand value
- Make the product remarkable
- Provide more value to your customers

Anything that can't be placed into one of these categories should not be considered of value. The idea is that a feature's justification should be traceable to one or more of the categories above by asking "why?" a few times.

We've discussed before the concept of the cost of testing versus the benefits we get from it. Our concern was to make sure that we didn't waste time on tests that didn't really provide much value to our code quality. Similarly, BDD strives to ensure the software's features as a whole provide real business value that justifies the cost of development. Making cost/benefit analysis the most important consideration in software development is, in my opinion, BDD's main contribution.

However, it is quite hard in practice to justify business value within our tests. Looking at real-world examples of BDD, including the Cucumber feature files for RSpec and Cucumber, one finds few clear justifications of business value. Instead, there are specifications of behavior such as we would accept in an outside-in acceptance test. We'll save ourselves a lot of time and frustration by taking note of this particular detail of how BDD in the real world diverges from its formal definition. We will still pay attention to justifying the value of the features we develop with BDD, but we won't go overboard by overthinking the justification or by forcing the reasoning into the tests themselves.

MMFs by example

We'll be developing an app that manages a todo list. Let's develop an MMF for the app. The MMF is an important element of organizing our specification in BDD. First, let's start with the justification of value. The common structure for these justifications is in three parts:

```
As a …
In order to …
I want to …
```

The idea is to specify the role of the user first. Then we write what the value is to that user. Finally, we describe how the user achieves that value. The feature itself is only in the last part, but the first two parts provide important context. We can also expand each part to have multiple declarations, simply by using the conjunction `and`.

Without further delay, let's write a justification for a **todo list manager** app:

```
As a user
In order to keep track of what I need to do
And in order to keep track of what I've already finished
I want to add todo items to a list
And I want to mark them as completed
```

The preceding description seems obvious and not remarkable. We'll work on improving it. But first, let's look again at the structure. The first sentence specifies the role of the person using the feature. We've defined the role as `user`, which is very generic and doesn't shed much light on who this feature is really aimed at.

The next two lines specify the value. We've given a little bit of detail, but it's somewhat vague and repetitive. We'll have to improve this.

The last two lines specify the two main features of a todo list manager: adding an item and marking it as completed. This is good. We could have added more detail, such as `I want to see my list of items`, but that is already assumed. In general, we don't want to be exhaustive with every single thing that the feature does. Rather, we want to highlight the important parts.

Let's work on improving the justification by first thinking about the role of the person using the system. We could come up with some ideas about what kind of person would benefit from a todo list manager app. Perhaps someone who is busy, or somebody who likes to be very organized. There aren't any obvious answers here. The point is to clarify for a particular team, organization, or engineer, who the software is intended for. A todo list manager could be useful to a college student managing assignments, an office worker managing tasks, a parent managing errands, or a supermarket shopper managing a shopping list. We may wind up with slightly different variations for different kinds of users. For example, we may add price and quantity fields for shoppers. For college students, we may add a field for the due date of an assignment.

Another important thing to consider is that the role can change over time. We may start out with an app geared toward college students, then find that it has become popular with office workers. BDD can help us to evolve our feature and its justification as our app's users change.

For now, let's choose the role of the office worker, since that fits the use case of a generic todo list well.

Now, let's move on to the value proposition. The role of office worker can help us right away to make this part more specific. For an office worker, the todo list is a way to make sure that all tasks get done. Another important value is knowing what has not been done. If we had chosen the role of college student, we would have had to also consider due dates, which tend to be much more rigid in academic environments than in companies. We can also imagine that the office worker's manager may be interested in the todo list, but in a different way. For the manager, the todo list provides value by showing how efficient the office worker is, so aggregate values such as number of tasks completed and percentage of tasks completed are more important. We can see that reflecting on the role and the value proposition can shed a lot of light on what we develop and for whom.

We won't go into the actual decision of which is more valuable. That is a difficult and context-specific topic, and as we mentioned earlier, it is not realistic for this kind of judgment to always be embedded explicitly in our BDD spec.

Here's what our updated MMF looks like:

```
As an office worker
In order to make sure I finish all my tasks for the day
And in order to know which tasks are still outstanding
I want to add todo items to a list
And I want to mark them as completed
```

One last note before we move on to writing our actual specs. We could have moved the second value proposition into a feature at the end. This kind of issue comes up often when dealing with BDD. It is really a matter of emphasis and the level of generalization we are comfortable with. Here, I've chosen to highlight the value of knowing which tasks are not yet finished. If the feature itself was something special, we could have highlighted a feature that would show unfinished tasks instead. Again, this is an area where there aren't obvious right or wrong answers.

Using TodoMVC

We'll build a todo list manager based on the **TodoMVC** application (`http://todomvc.com`). This simple, open source application with a rich JavaScript user interface will provide plenty of behavior to specify with BDD. Our implementation will be simpler than the full TodoMVC app, but we'll make sure that our BDD features will work on the full app as well. This will demonstrate how acceptance tests can target both local and deployed instances of an app; in this case, different implementations.

We will first define our feature in a BDD-style RSpec example. Then we'll execute our feature file, which will fail since we won't have any code at that point. We'll then iterate through the development process, building the user interface first, with no Ruby backend. Then we'll move in steps to developing our controller, or API layer, using TDD. Finally, we'll build the model layer that powers our API.

It's important to note that the BDD process is very free flowing, with a natural bouncing back and forth between features, app code, and specs. This flow is not easy to capture in the format of a book chapter. In the sections to come, we will try to follow a clear, logical course through the development of our app. This does not mean that real-world experience with BDD is meant to be linear and logical. The whole point of BDD is to enable experimentation with different ideas throughout the development process to maximize benefit while minimizing cost. As we work through the example app and its features, we should use our imagination to consider alternative directions along the way.

Specifying the MMF

Let's start with the two simplest features of a todo list manager: adding items and marking them as completed. We'll also need some support code to set up our specs. Keep in mind that these specs should serve as documentation for the high-level behavior of the todo list manager so it shouldn't look too much like code. Here it is, in a file called `todo_feature.rb`, located in the `spec/features` folder. Note that we didn't use the usual convention of ending the file name with `_spec.rb` since we want to differentiate this from our normal specs:

```
require_relative '../feature_helper'

RSpec.feature "Manage to-do items", :type => :feature do

    # As an office worker
    # In order to make sure I finish all my tasks for the day
    # And in order to know which tasks are still outstanding
    # I want to add todo items to a list
    # And I want to mark them as completed

  include WebInputHelpers

  before(:example) { reset_page }

  scenario "add" do
    add_item "Learn Go"
    add_item "Review C"
```

```
    expect(page).to have_content 'Learn Go'
    expect(page).to have_content 'Review C'

    expect(page).to have_content '2 items left'
  end

  scenario 'mark as done' do
    add_item "Learn Go"
    add_item "Review C"

    expect(page).to have_content 'Learn Go'
    expect(page).to have_content 'Review C'

    expect(page).to have_content '2 items left'

    check_item 'Review C'

    expect(page).to have_completed_item 'Review C'
    expect(page).to_not have_completed_item 'Learn Go'

    expect(page).to have_content '1 item left'
  end
end
```

You'll notice we use `feature` instead of `describe` and `scenario` instead of `it`. These are simply aliases to give our BDD spec more of a documentation flavor. We've used a few custom helpers and a custom matcher here. These are made available to our feature code due to the `include WebInputHelpers` line. The `WebInputHelpers` module is loaded when we require `feature_helper` on the first line of the feature. Before we look into how these are defined, let's look at our feature more closely.

We can see that the actions and assertions are more or less in plain language. Even though we don't know the definition of `reset_page`, `add_item`, or `have_completed_item`, we know what their intent is just by their names. These methods all interact with the HTML markup of our UI using Capybara's DSL. It's easy to just skip this step of defining custom helpers, but that would quickly make it impossible for our feature to serve the purpose of clearly documenting the behavior of our app with an example. Look at the definition of `reset_page`, for example:

```
def reset_page
  visit '/'

  if page.has_selector?('input[type=checkbox]')
    all('input[type=checkbox]').first.click
    click_on 'Clear completed'
  end
end
```

If we had this in our `before` block, it would be hard to know what it was there for. The CSS selectors used to find elements are not at all readable and if we replaced `add_item` and `have_completed_item` with similar CSS-heavy method calls, our BDD feature would turn into a simple acceptance test. Would that be so bad? It's certainly not the end of the world, but one of the benefits of BDD is to help to specify a domain language for our feature. In this case, we have a pretty simple feature, but as an app gets bigger, we find it hard to find clear, meaningful terms to describe the behavior of the app. We wind up using overly specific language that is full of technical detail and lose sight of the purpose of the feature. Remember that BDD is about defining the right feature, not just any feature. To do that effectively, we need a clear, simple language in order to talk about our features without any excess technical detail.

Configuring RSpec to run a feature file

Let's have a look now at `spec/feature_helper.rb`, which will load all of the setup code, helpers, and custom matchers. This is what that file contains:

```
require_relative 'config/common'
require_relative 'config/capybara'
require_relative 'helpers/web_input_helpers'
require_relative 'helpers/custom_matchers'
```

It's just a little wrapper that pulls in four different files. We've kept everything nice and clean by using separate files for each concern. This will help keep our RSpec code maintainable and will make it easier to follow changes as our feature evolves over the course of this and the following chapter.

We have first a little file called `spec/config/capybara.rb` with some basic RSpec configuration:

```
RSpec.configure do |config|
  config.color = true
end
```

Let's look at the next file that we load, `spec/config/capybara.rb`:

```
require 'capybara/rspec'

Capybara.default_driver = :selenium

if ENV['APP_HOST'] == 'local'
  puts 'Booting a local server using config.ru...'

  # use config.ru to boot the rack app
```

```
    config_ru   = File.expand_path('../../../config.ru', __FILE__)
    Capybara.app = Rack::Builder.parse_file(config_ru).first
  else
    # configure Capybara
    DEFAULT_APP_HOST   = 'http://localhost:9292'

    Capybara.run_server = false
    Capybara.app_host   = ENV['APP_HOST'] || DEFAULT_APP_HOST
  end
```

We won't go into detail here about the Capybara configuration. Basically, we're able
to set the APP_HOST environment variable to control the target URL for our features.
This is important for allowing us to test local development as well as deployed
versions of our app. There's a special value of local for APP_HOST which will boot
up a Rack web app based on the file config.ru, which we will discuss shortly.

Next, let's look at spec/helpers/web_input_helpers.rb:

```
# helpers to encapsulate CSS & HTML navigation
module WebInputHelpers
  def reset_page
    visit '/'

    if page.has_selector?('input[type=checkbox]')
      all('input[type=checkbox]').first.click
      click_on 'Clear completed'
    end
  end

  def add_item(s)
    # add a newline to simulate pressing enter in the UI
    # this may not work with all browsers
    # alternative: find('#new-todo').native.send_keys(:return)
    s_with_newline = s.strip + "\n"

    fill_in "What needs to be done?", :with => s_with_newline
  end

  def check_item(s)
    items = all('#todo-list li')

    if items.size == 0
      fail 'No todos found'
    end
```

```
        # iterate over each todo item
        items.select do |node|
          # click the checkbox for the matching item
          if node.text == s
            node.find('input[type=checkbox]').click
          end
        end
    end

    def screenshot(name=nil)
      name ||= 'screenshot' + Time.now.to_i.to_s + '.png'

      page.save_screenshot(name)
    end
  end
```

Here we've defined our custom methods to interact with the page and check its assertions. It takes quite a bit of trial and error to come up with the right CSS selectors for these helpers. This is a place where you'll have to use your imagination to think through how you'd start off your feature definition when you don't have any code at all. Probably, you'd use many more generic selectors based on text. I've used the structure of the markup in the TodoMVC app, which shortcuts the process. One point of difficulty is often that simple text is repeated throughout the page, and more complex selectors are needed to get the exact element that is being targeted. There are also some odd little tricks, such as the way we use a final newline character for the add_item method to simulate a user pressing the *Enter* button. Similar issues come up with file upload dialogs, alert windows, and other interactive browser behaviors.

One other piece of RSpec code we'll look at before running our feature is spec/helpers/custom_matchers.rb:

```
require 'rspec/expectations'

# custom matchers to simplify assertions
RSpec::Matchers.define :have_completed_item do |text|
  match do |node|
    node.has_selector?('.completed label', :text => text)
  end

  match_when_negated do |node|
    node.has_no_selector?('.completed label', :text => text)
  end
end
```

Here we use Capybara's `has_selector?` and `has_no_selector?` methods along with a little CSS to define a new `have_completed_item` matcher. The only new thing here is the combination of custom matchers, which we learned about in *Chapter 2*, *Specifying Behavior with Examples and Matchers*, with Capybara's DSL, which we learned about in *Chapter 6*, *Driving a Web Browser with Capybara*.

The last thing we need to deal with is the installation of the required Ruby gems so our feature is runnable. So far we've just used the `gem` command to install gems one by one. This is fine for trying things out, but to build a real app, we need to use a proper gem manager. We'll use **Bundler** (`http://bundler.io`), which is by far the most popular gem manager. We'll have to run `gem install bundler` from the command line to install `bundler`, then we simply create a file named `Gemfile` in the root folder of our app (alongside the `spec` folder) listing the gems we'll need:

```
source 'https://rubygems.org'

gem 'rack'

group :test do
  gem 'rspec'
  gem 'capybara'
  gem 'selenium-webdriver'
end
```

The last step is to run `bundle install` from the command line to install all of the required gems.

The BDD process begins

Now let's run the feature. We can't get too excited yet since we expect our tests to all fail. We haven't written any code, after all, but we can confirm that we've got everything configured properly and get started with the BDD process. Let's run our feature for the first time:

```
                              Terminal
$ APP_HOST=http://localhost:9292 rspec spec/**/*_feature.rb
FF

Failures:

  1) Manage to-do items add
     Failure/Error: fill_in "What needs to be done?", :with => s_with_newline

     Capybara::ElementNotFound:
       Unable to find field "What needs to be done?"
```

I've only shown the top part of the output for the sake of brevity. While the feature was running, you should also have seen Mozilla Firefox launch and display an error message before it closed itself:

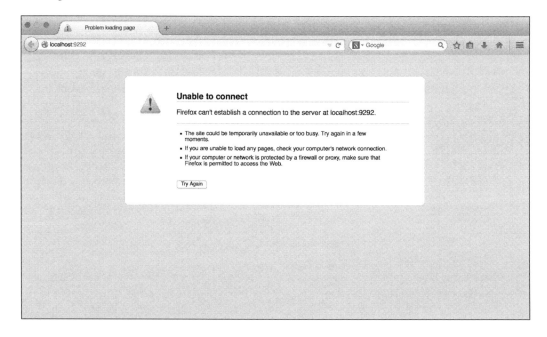

Not very impressive. Note that we set APP_HOST to the apparently random value of http://localhost:9292 and since we have no web server running at that URL, or even any code that could be run yet, it makes sense that we got a failure. Another point to pay attention to is that Capybara's error message was as follows:

```
Unable to find field "What needs to be done?"
```

It would have been nice for Capybara to tell us that the browser was not able to even connect to the URL we supplied, but the error message can be confusing. It would have been the same message if there was a server running but that particular line of text was not found.

Building web apps with Rack

Now we're finally ready to write some code. We'll start building our view with HTML and JavaScript, working our way from the outside in. We're going to have to speed through this first step as it is impossible to capture the chaotic first steps of building a UI. The main point to keep in mind is that we're skipping the Ruby code that will power our app eventually.

We'll have a tiny mock web app in Ruby that serves our static HTML and JavaScript files, but that doesn't really count. By defining our UI first, we can figure out what our remaining code will need to do.

First, let's get our mock web app out of the way. All this does is serve static files, and we could have used **Nginx** or any other web server to achieve the same result. But we're going to use **Rack** (http://rack.github.io), a popular Ruby web server interface. It's worth learning more about Rack, as it's one of the most important Ruby libraries out there, and is the foundation of Sinatra, Rails, and other popular Ruby web libraries.

First, let's start with a tiny Rack web app so we get the basics of how Rack works. Here is the file for our app, tiny_rack_app.rb:

```ruby
require 'rack'

# A Rack app is any ruby object that responds to the 'call' method...
# ... in this case an instance of the TinyRackApp
class TinyRackApp
  def call(env)
    [
      200,                             # HTTP status
      {'Content-type' => 'text/plain'}, # HTTP headers
      [ "Hello", ", ", "World", "!" ]   # HTTP body, in chunks
    ]
  end
end

# if this file was executed directly, start the Rack app
if __FILE__ == $0
  Rack::Handler::WEBrick.run TinyRackApp.new
end
```

We'll explain the code in a moment. First, let's start the app and send it a request to see how it works. Make sure you've installed the Rack gem (gem install rack). Then you can start the app in the terminal very simply:

```
$ ruby tiny_rack_app.rb
[2015-12-07 22:38:51] INFO  WEBrick 1.3.1 [2015-12-07 22:38:51] INFO
ruby 2.2.0 (2014-12-25) [x86_64-darwin14]
[2015-12-07 22:38:51] INFO  WEBrick::HTTPServer#start: pid=19223
port=8080
```

Using a web browser, go to `http://localhost:8080` and you'll see a response of `Hello, World!`. If you want to see more detail, you can open another terminal window and send a request with `curl`:

```
$ curl --verbose http://localhost:8080
* Rebuilt URL to: http://localhost:8080/
*    Trying ::1...
* Connected to localhost (::1) port 8080 (#0)
> GET / HTTP/1.1
> Host: localhost:8080
> User-Agent: curl/7.43.0
> Accept: */*
>
< HTTP/1.1 200 OK
< Content-Type: text/plain
< Server: WEBrick/1.3.1 (Ruby/2.2.0/2014-12-25)
< Date: Tue, 08 Dec 2015 06:50:51 GMT
< Content-Length: 13
< Connection: Keep-Alive
<
* Connection #0 to host localhost left intact
Hello, World!
```

Notice the `Content-Type: text/plain` header in the response.

If we look back at the code, we see there isn't much to a Rack application. Of course, this app is just an example that always returns the same response, which we've hardcoded in the `TinyRackApp#call` method. But an entire Sinatra app is still just a Rack application that returns, after all of its processing, a simple array of three items:

- HTTP status code as an integer (in this case, `200`)
- HTTP headers as a Hash (in this case, `Content-type: text/plain`)
- HTTP body as an object that responds to the `each` method (in this case the array of String that add up to `Hello, World!`)

We won't go into too much detail, but note that the body is not a simple String but rather an array. This is because an HTTP body can be very long and processing it is much more efficient if it can be handled in chunks. Note that the HTTP body in the response is simply `Hello, World!`. The only reason we've split that up into multiple elements is to illustrate this point. In future examples, we'll just use a one-element array with the body as one String.

One last thing to note is that we start the Rack application in the file itself by calling `Rack::Handler::WEBrick.run` when the files is executed directly (in other words, when we run `ruby tiny_rack_app.rb`). This is the simplest way to start up a Rack application, but it's not very practical in the real world, where we would never want to limit ourselves to a single web server (and definitely not the very slow `WEBrick`).

Serving static files using Rack middleware

Middleware is one of the most useful tools in Rack. With middleware, we can create an intermediate mini-application that receives an HTTP request before our main web app to do some work based on the request's headers, body, and HTTP method.

The term "do some work" is very vague. Indeed, we can do just about anything with Rack middleware. Here we are simply going to serve static files using the `Rack::Static` middleware that comes with Rack.

In our simple example, we started Rack from within our app file, using `Rack::Handler::WEBrick.run`. That's not usually how Rack apps are configured. Normally there is a separate file to manage the start of the Rack application. By convention, this file is always called `config.ru`, although it is a normal Ruby file. In our case, we will have the following code in `config.ru`:

```
require 'bundler/setup'
require 'rack/builder'

require_relative 'dummy_app'

NoBackendTodoApp = Rack::Builder.new do
  # Serve all requests to /static as static assets
  use Rack::Static, :urls => ["/static"]

  # Serve any requests to '/index.html' with '/static/index.html'
  use Rack::Static,
    :urls  => ["index.html"],
    :root  => 'static',
    :index => 'index.html'

  map '/api/v1' do
    run DummyApp.new
  end
end

run NoBackendTodoApp
```

We've defined an app that will serve files from the static folder and then respond with dummy text at the path /api/v1, based on what we've defined in dummy_app.rb, which contains the following:

```
class DummyApp
  def call(*args)
    [ 200, {}, ["API v1"] ]
  end
end
```

We'll use the rackup command as before to start up the web server. This command looks for config.ru by default. Then we'll make a request to the app using curl:

```
● ● ●                                    Terminal
$ rackup
[2016-02-29 21:29:15] INFO  WEBrick 1.3.1
[2016-02-29 21:29:15] INFO  ruby 2.2.0 (2014-12-25) [x86_64-darwin14]
[2016-02-29 21:29:15] INFO  WEBrick::HTTPServer#start: pid=71994 port=9292
::1 - - [29/Feb/2016:21:29:17 -0800] "GET /api/v1 HTTP/1.1" 200 - 0.0056
```

You can see the next-to-last line of the output shows us that the server is listening on port 9292 (the default port where Rack apps run and the explanation for the apparently random URL we used before, http://localhost:9292). The last line is showing us that Rack received a GET request and responded with status 200. Here's the request and response:

```
● ● ●                                    Terminal
$ curl -v http://localhost:9292/api/v1
*   Trying ::1...
* Connected to localhost (::1) port 9292 (#0)
> GET /api/v1 HTTP/1.1
> Host: localhost:9292
> User-Agent: curl/7.43.0
> Accept: */*
>
< HTTP/1.1 200 OK
< Transfer-Encoding: chunked
< Server: WEBrick/1.3.1 (Ruby/2.2.0/2014-12-25)
< Date: Tue, 01 Mar 2016 05:29:17 GMT
< Connection: Keep-Alive
<
* Connection #0 to host localhost left intact
API v1
$
```

Now that we've got a feature file and a way to serve static assets, we're ready to start building our todo list manager from the outside in, which will be our focus in *Chapter 8, Tackling the Challenges of End-to-end Testing*, where we build on the foundations we laid in this chapter.

Summary

In this chapter we delved into BDD with Capybara. We learned how BDD focuses on specifying behavior and acts more like documentation than tests. We also learned some basics about Rack and how to serve static assets with it.

8
Tackling the Challenges of End-to-end Testing

In *Chapter 7, Building an App from the Outside In with Behavior-Driven Development*, we learned about BDD and wrote a feature file to define the behavior of a small web app. Now we are going to build our todo list manager. We'll start with a rich JavaScript UI defined in AngularJS, then move on to the TDD of a backend API and model. We'll discuss some of the difficulties of BDD along with some ideas for how to take advantage of its benefits while avoiding its pitfalls. We'll end with an initial implementation of authentication middleware for our API using JSON Web Token.

Here are some of the things we'll learn in this chapter:

- Iterating between acceptance tests and application code
- Building a rich JavaScript web UI with AngularJS
- Testing UI interactions with a rich web app
- Using Rack middleware for authentication

Step 1 – building the view

First, let's create the static files that will define our UI. We learned how to serve these files using Rack in *Chapter 7, Building an App from the Outside In with Behavior-Driven Development*.

First, here's `static/index.html`:

```html
<!doctype html>
<html ng-app="todoApp">
<head>
  <script src="/static/vendor/angularjs/angular.js">
  </script>

  <script src="/static/js/mock_todo_list.js">
  </script>

  <script src="/static/js/todo_list_controller.js">
  </script>

  <script src="/static/js/app.js">
  </script>

  <style>
  .completed label {
    text-decoration: line-through;
    color: grey;
  }

  #todo-list li {
    list-style-image: none;
    list-style-position: outside;
    list-style-type: none;
  }
  </style>
</head>
<body>
  <h2>Todo List Manager</h2>

  <section ng-controller="TodoListController">

    <div>
      <!-- useful for debugging
        <pre><code>{{todos | json}}</code></pre>
      -->

      <form name="todo-list-form" ng-submit="addTodo()">
        <fieldset>
          <legend ng-switch on="todos.length">
            <span ng-switch-when="0">
```

```
          Enter an item
        </span>
        <span ng-switch-default>
          <ng-pluralize count="unfinishedCount"
          when="{'1': '{} item','other': '{} items'}">
        </ng-pluralize>
        left
        ({{todos.length}} total)
      </span>
    </legend>

    <input
    name="new-todo"
    type="text"
    ng-model="newTodoText"
    placeholder="What needs to be done?"
    >
    <input type="submit" value="add">

    <button type="button" ng-click="clearCompleted()" ng-
show="todos.length">
        Clear completed
    </button>
  </fieldset>
</form>

<ul id="todo-list">
  <li
  ng-repeat="todo in todos"
  ng-class="{completed: todo.done}"
  >

  <label>
    <input
    type="checkbox"
    ng-model="todo.done"
    ng-change="toggleDone(todo)"
    >
    {{todo.text}}
  </label>
  </li>
</ul>

</section>
</body>
</html>
```

We're using AngularJS to power our rich JavaScript UI. Don't worry though. Our code is so simple, it is about the same as the second example on the AngularJS home page (`https://angularjs.org`). We won't spend any time explaining the view but will rush through the rest of the static files that are loaded by `index.html`. First, we load the AngularJS library itself (version 1.5.0). Then we load `static/js/mock_todo_list.js`, which is a service that handles the data manipulation for our todo list manager. Here's what that file looks like:

```
'use strict';

// define the model to handle the data
var MockTodoList = function () {
  var store = {
    todos: []
  };

  store.all = function(){
    return this.todos;
  }

  store.add = function(todoText){
    var newTodo = {"text" : todoText, "done" : false};

    this.todos.push(newTodo);

    return newTodo;
  }

  store.unfinished = function(){
    return this.todos.filter(function(todo) {
      return (! todo.done)
    });
  }

  store.deleteAll = function() {
    this.todos = [];
    return this.todos;
  }

  store.deleteCompleted = function(){
    this.todos = this.unfinished();

    return this.todos;
  }

  return store;
};
```

Next, we load `static/js/todo_list_controller.js`, which links our view with the AngularJS code we've defined. The methods and variables we used in `index.html` are defined in this controller. Here's what that file contains:

```
'use strict';

// define the angular controller to connect the model to the view
var TodoListController = function($scope, TodoList) {
  $scope.todos = TodoList.all();

  $scope.addTodo = function() {
    if ( (typeof $scope.newTodoText === 'string') && $scope.
newTodoText.length > 0)  {
      TodoList.add($scope.newTodoText);
      $scope.newTodoText = '';
      $scope.todos = TodoList.all();
    }
  };

  $scope.$watchCollection('todos', function(newVal){
    if (newVal){
      $scope.unfinishedCount = newVal.filter(function(todo){
        return ! todo.done;
      }).length
    }
  });

  $scope.clearCompleted = function() {
    $scope.todos = TodoList.deleteCompleted();
  };

  $scope.toggleDone = function(todo){
    if (todo.done) {
      $scope.unfinishedCount = $scope.unfinishedCount - 1;
    } else {
      $scope.unfinishedCount = $scope.unfinishedCount + 1;
    }
  };
};
```

Finally, we have `static/js/app.js`, which initializes the AngularJS app so everything works. Here are its contents:

```
'use strict';

angular.module('todoApp', [])
  .factory('TodoList', MockTodoList)
  .controller('TodoListController', [
    '$scope',
    'TodoList',
    TodoListController
  ]);
;
```

Now that we've added these files, we can use a browser to try out our UI. Make sure that `rackup` is still running and then navigate to `http://localhost:9292`. Here's what you should see:

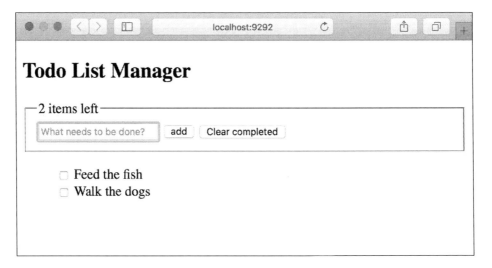

Take some time to try out the app. It should be pretty self-explanatory, but even a simple little app like this can have bugs. Once you've gotten a feel for how the app works, let's move on to run our `feature` file again. This time it should pass:

```
$ APP_HOST=http://localhost:9292 rspec spec/**/*_feature.rb
..

Finished in 6.72 seconds (files took 0.5479 seconds to load)
2 examples, 0 failures

$
```

And this time you should see the web app running inside Firefox instead of an error message:

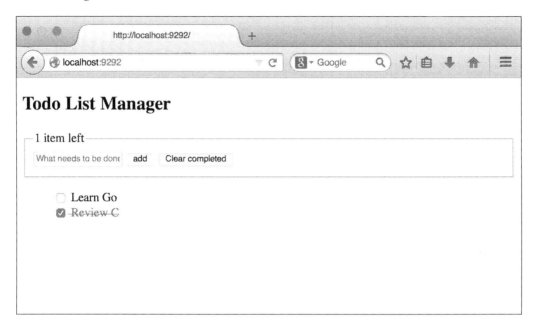

That's it, we've taken our first step into the world of BDD and we're already past the hardest part. Let's recall that our app has no storage or backend. Each time we reload the page, we lose any todos we had previously entered. In the next section, we'll add a backend to our app to add these important basic capabilities. Before you move on, make sure to review all the many parts to this simple app and its simple feature file. We'll build on this foundation for the rest of this chapter.

Step 2 – defining the API

We're going to add some backend code in Ruby so that we have an API server for our view to connect to. This will allow us to save our todo list between browser sessions. It will also lay the foundation for many new features that we might want to add in the real world, such as sharing lists with other people, user management, and sending e-mail reminders about unfinished todos.

So where do we start with our backend code? With BDD, we keep going from the outside in. We'll just make a small change to our AngularJS service to rely on an HTTP API. That will give us a list of endpoints that our API server needs to handle and a good starting place for our work on the backend. This is one of the benefits of BDD. It points the way to the exact code we need to write along the way, taking the guesswork out of where to start.

Let's replace `static/js/mock_todo_list.js` with `static/js/todo_list.js` with the following contents:

```
'use strict';

// define the model to handle the data
var TodoList = function ($http) {
  var store = {};

  function returnTodos(response){
    return response.data.todos;
  }

  store.all = function(){
    return $http.get('/api/v1/todos').then(returnTodos);
  }

  store.add = function(todoText){
    var newTodo = {"text" : todoText, "done" : false};

    return $http.post('/api/v1/todos', newTodo).then(returnTodos);
  }

  store.deleteAll = function() {
    return $http.delete('/api/v1/todos').then(returnTodos);
  }

  store.deleteCompleted = function(){
    return $http.delete('/api/v1/todos/done').then(returnTodos);
  }

  return store;
};
```

We'll skip the explanation of the AngularJS code above, but just note that all of our functions now use `$http` to get their info, which we can presume will make HTTP requests to the paths specified. We will also have to update `static/index.html` to replace the following line:

```
<script src="/static/js/mock_todo_list.js">
```

We'll update this as follows:

```
<script src="/static/js/todo_list.js">
```

Our controller file, `static/js/todo_list_controller.js`, also needs to change:

```javascript
'use strict';

// define the angular controller to connect the model to the view
var TodoListController = function($scope, TodoList) {
  TodoList.all().then(function(todos){
    $scope.todos = todos;
  });

  $scope.addTodo = function() {
    if ( (typeof $scope.newTodoText === 'string') && $scope.
newTodoText.length > 0)  {
      TodoList.add($scope.newTodoText).then(function(todos){
        $scope.newTodoText = '';

        $scope.todos = todos;
      });
    }
  };

  $scope.$watchCollection('todos', function(newVal){
    if (newVal){
      $scope.unfinishedCount = newVal.filter(function(todo){
        return ! todo.done;
      }).length
    }
  });

  $scope.clearCompleted = function() {
    TodoList.deleteCompleted().then(function(todos){
      $scope.todos = todos;
    });
  };

  $scope.toggleDone = function(todo){
    if (todo.done) {
      $scope.unfinishedCount = $scope.unfinishedCount - 1;
    } else {
      $scope.unfinishedCount = $scope.unfinishedCount + 1;
    }
  };
};
```

The main difference is that the calls to the `TodoList` service look more complicated. That is because an HTTP request is asynchronous and we have to wait for it to finish at some unspecified time in the future before we have the return value that we need. We're using AngularJS's Promise interface here with the `then()` method to wait for the HTTP request to succeed before we set the return value.

Finally, there are a couple of small changes to `static/js/app.js` in order to load the new service properly:

```
'use strict';

angular.module('todoApp', [])
  .factory('TodoList', [
    '$http',
    TodoList
  ])
  .controller('TodoListController', [
    '$scope',
    'TodoList',
    TodoListController
  ]);
;
```

You can try out the page now in a browser if you like. Nothing will work since we haven't defined any of our endpoints. If we run our feature file again, then we'll get failures for both features we've defined. It seems like we've taken a step back by going from passing features to failing features. But that is a natural part of the development process. The main point to keep in mind is that our features systematically let us know when our whole app is working or not, reducing our reliance on manual testing and guesswork.

Based on our AngularJS service, we know we need to implement four HTTP endpoints:

- `GET /api/v1/todos` to retrieve the list of all todos
- `POST /api/v1/todos` to add a new todo item
- `DELETE /api/v1/todos` to delete all todos
- `DELETE /api/v1/todos/finished` to delete finished todos

At this point in the BDD flow, we switch gears to TDD to write some tests for our new API even before we write any code for it. Strictly speaking, we could have done the same thing for our AngularJS code, but that would be outside the scope of this book. For API or controller tests, we won't use the full outside-in, black-box approach. Instead we'll use functional tests, which are somewhere in between black-box tests and unit tests. This will allow us to easily write tests for API endpoints that are reasonably realistic.

```
ENV['RACK_ENV'] = 'test'

require_relative 'config/common'
require_relative '../app'
require 'rspec'
require 'rack/test'

module RackTestBrowser
  extend self

  def new_browser
    app = Todo::API
    Rack::Test::Session.new(Rack::MockSession.new(app))
  end
end
```

We're going to use `Rack::Test` for the API specs, and here we're requiring the library and creating a little helper module to give us a new instance of a "browser", which is not actually doing HTTP requests, but simulating them. This makes `Rack::Test` fast and easy to use. But there are some drawbacks to this approach, as certain behaviors will not be the same. We'll discuss these issues later in this chapter.

Now let's look our new `app.rb`:

```
require 'sinatra/base'

module Todo
  class API < Sinatra::Base
  end
end
```

We're now using `Sinatra` to build our API (`http://www.sinatrarb.com`). Sinatra is a minimal DSL for creating web applications built on top of Rack and will allow us to easily define our new endpoints. We could have continued to use plain Rack, but that makes defining paths and responses cumbersome.

Now let's create a little spec file at `spec/api/todo_api_spec.rb`:

```
require_relative '../api_helper'

RSpec.describe Todo::API, api: true do
  # create a new browser session before each example
```

```
    let!(:browser) { RackTestBrowser.new_browser }

    context 'GET /api/v1/todos' do
      it 'returns an empty array at first' do
        browser.get '/api/v1/todos'

        expect(browser.last_response.status).to eq(200)
        expect(browser.last_response.body).to eq('[]')
      end
    end
  end
```

Before we run anything, let's make sure we have all of the gems we need installed.
Let's update our Gemfile to look like this:

```
source 'https://rubygems.org'

gem 'rack'
gem 'sinatra'
gem 'rack-parser'
gem 'sinatra'

gem 'multi_json'
gem 'redis'

group :test do
  gem 'rspec'
  gem 'capybara'
  gem 'selenium-webdriver'
end
```

Then we'll run bundle install on the command line to get any missing gems.

Now let's run this API spec and see what we get:

```
● ● ●                           Terminal
$ rspec spec/api/todo_api_spec.rb
F

Failures:

  1) Todo::API GET /api/v1/todos returns an empty array at first
     Failure/Error: expect(browser.last_response.status).to eq(200)

        expected: 200
             got: 404

        (compared using ==)
     # ./spec/api/todo_api_spec.rb:11:in `block (3 levels) in <top (required)>'

Finished in 0.03354 seconds (files took 0.21944 seconds to load)
1 example, 1 failure

Failed examples:

rspec ./spec/api/todo_api_spec.rb:8 # Todo::API GET /api/v1/todos returns an emp
ty array at first

$ ▌
```

Although the test fails, the error is encouraging. We got a `404` HTTP status code, which means the endpoint was not found. This is good, as all we have to do is define the endpoint in `Todo::API`, like so:

```ruby
require 'sinatra/base'
require 'multi_json'

module Todo
  class API < Sinatra::Base
    get '/api/v1/todos' do
      todos = []
      MultiJson.encode(todos)
    end
  end
end
```

The Sinatra DSL is self-explanatory. We've defined a `get` endpoint at the path `/api/v1/todos` and returned an empty array encoded as JSON using the `MultiJson` gem. Let's run the spec again and watch it pass:

```
● ● ●                           Terminal
$ rspec spec/api/todo_api_spec.rb
.

Finished in 0.03666 seconds (files took 0.21657 seconds to load)
1 example, 0 failures

$ ▊
```

That's progress, but we've got our todo list hardcoded as an empty array. It's clear we'll need to have some kind of code to manage the todo list. Let's just create the interface that's most convenient to use in our endpoint code and worry about the implementation later. While we're at it, let's add definitions for the other three endpoints as well:

```ruby
require 'sinatra/base'
require 'multi_json'

require_relative 'lib/todo_list'

module Todo
end

class Todo::API < Sinatra::Base
  get '/api/v1/todos' do
    todos = Todo::TodoList.all
    MultiJson.encode(todos)
  end

  post '/api/v1/todos' do
    Todo::TodoList.add(params)
    todos = Todo::TodoList.all
    MultiJson.encode(todos)
  end

  delete '/api/v1/todos' do
    response = Todo::TodoList.delete_all
    MultiJson.encode(response)
  end

  delete '/api/v1/todos/finished' do
    response = Todo::TodoList.delete_finished
    MultiJson.encode(response)
  end
end
```

And `'lib/todo_list.rb'` has a simple module definition for now:

```
module Todo
end

module Todo::TodoList
end
```

This is pretty straightforward, and just as the AngularJS service pointed us to the API endpoints we needed, we are now pointed to the `Todo::TodoList` model we'll need. This flow comes with BDD but it doesn't work for everything. At this point, we'll have to think about how we want to implement the model. Do we need a database? Can we just store the list in memory? For the purposes of our app, anything will work, but in the real world, early decisions like these can seriously constrain future options. Although BDD isn't going to directly help us make a choice, it does indirectly help by encouraging us to write features and tests at multiple levels. Having these will make our code more modular so that it is easier to make changes such as using a different database to store the list. We'll also be able to tell more easily when there is a problem by relying on our automated features and tests.

We know from our API code that we'll need four methods in the `Todo::TodoList` model:

- `Todo::TodoList.all` to get all todo items
- `Todo::TodoList.add` to add a todo item
- `Todo::TodoList.delete_all` to delete all todo items
- `Todo::TodoList.delete_finished` to delete only finished todo items

Let's use Redis as our backend store for the items. It's fast and lightweight enough to not get in the way, but its features and performance will make it adaptable to ever-growing demands. This kind of decision is very important. Although it's impossible to make the perfect decision early on about which component to use, with experience and reflection, we can learn to make very good decisions that don't lock in overly complex but powerful tools early on while avoiding toy tools that will crumple in the face of real-world usage. Again, this is an area where BDD doesn't directly help us. We have to rely on our own experience and judgment for the most part.

We haven't finished with our API specs but it's clear that they won't work without an implementation of `Todo::TodoList`. We could mock all of the calls to `Todo::TodoList` in our API specs, but for such a simple API and model, that doesn't make sense. So let's skip ahead to implementing `Todo::TodoList` the TDD way, by writing tests first.

Given our choice of Redis, we'll need a way to let the model know about the Redis client connection. In *Chapter 4, Setting Up and Cleaning Up* and *Chapter 5, Simulating External Services*, we used a global constant to store our Redis client connection and referred to it directly in our code. That's not the best way of doing things. It's more modular to allow the connection to be passed in. To that end, we should use a class to implement `Todo::TodoList` instead of a module so that we have an initialization step.

Let's start off with our first spec in `spec/lib/todo_list_spec.rb`:

```
require_relative '../spec_helper'
require_relative '../../lib/todo_list'

RSpec.describe Todo::TodoList, redis: true do
  context '.new' do
    it 'expects a Redis client' do
      expect{
        described_class.new(:foo)
      }.to raise_error('Expected a Redis instance, got Symbol')
    end

    it 'sets @redis_client' do
      tl = described_class.new(::REDIS_CLIENT)

      actual = tl.instance_variable_get(:@redis_client)

      expect(actual).to eq(::REDIS_CLIENT)
    end
  end
end
```

You'll notice that we're now relying on a `spec/spec_helper.rb` file, which has the following contents:

```
require 'rspec'
require_relative 'config/common'
require_relative '../initializers/redis'

RSpec.configure do |config|
  if ! defined?(::REDIS_CLIENT)
    raise("No REDIS_CLIENT defined!")
  end

  config.before(:example, :redis) do
    ::REDIS_CLIENT.flushdb
  end

  config.after(:example, :redis) do
```

```
        ::REDIS_CLIENT.flushdb
    end
end
```

This is similar to what we saw in *Chapter 4*, *Setting Up and Cleaning Up* and *Chapter 5*, *Simulating External Services*, except that we're now flushing the database before and after our specs. We've already seen `spec/config/common.rb`, so let's look at the new file in `initializers/redis.rb`:

```ruby
require 'redis'

ENV['REDIS_URL'] ||= 'redis://localhost:6379/15'

if ! ENV['REDIS_URL'].is_a?(String)
  raise "REDIS_URL environment variable not set"
end

::REDIS_CLIENT = Redis.new( :url => ENV['REDIS_URL'] )
```

The Redis initialization code is now all in this file, allowing us to use it in both our specs and our code. Following our pattern, let's run our spec file before we update `Todo::TodoList`:

```
. . .                              Terminal
$ rspec spec/lib/todo_list_spec.rb
FF

Failures:

  1) Todo::TodoList.new expects a Redis client
     Failure/Error:
       expect{
         described_class.new(:foo)
       }.to raise_error('Expected a Redis instance, got Symbol')

       expected Exception with "Expected a Redis instance, got Symbol", got #<No
MethodError: undefined method `new' for Todo::TodoList:Module> with backtrace:
         # ./spec/lib/todo_list_spec.rb:8:in `block (4 levels) in <top (required
)>'
         # ./spec/lib/todo_list_spec.rb:7:in `block (3 levels) in <top (required
)>'
       # ./spec/lib/todo_list_spec.rb:7:in `block (3 levels) in <top (required)>'

  2) Todo::TodoList.new sets @redis_client
     Failure/Error: tl = described_class.new(::REDIS_CLIENT)

     NoMethodError:
       undefined method `new' for Todo::TodoList:Module
       # ./spec/lib/todo_list_spec.rb:13:in `block (3 levels) in <top (required)>'

Finished in 0.01471 seconds (files took 0.13001 seconds to load)
2 examples, 2 failures

Failed examples:

rspec ./spec/lib/todo_list_spec.rb:6 # Todo::TodoList.new expects a Redis client
rspec ./spec/lib/todo_list_spec.rb:12 # Todo::TodoList.new sets @redis_client

$ 
```

The errors tell us what we already know, that we have a module, but are trying to call new on it like a class. Let's change lib/todo_list.rb to look like this:

```
require 'redis'

module Todo
end

class Todo::TodoList
  def initialize(redis_client)
    if ! (redis_client.is_a?(Redis))
      raise "Expected a Redis instance, got #{redis_client.class}"
    end

    @redis_client = redis_client
  end
end
```

Now if we run our tests again with rspec spec/lib/todo_list_spec.rb, they should both pass. Let's move on to writing more specs. Which method should we start with? We have to be smart here to have a basic method tested first that we can then use in subsequent specs. This basic method can be tested by directly querying Redis to ensure it stores the data in the way we expect. The add method is the place to start, since we'll need to add some todos before we can get a list of all of them, or delete any of them. We could directly query Redis in all of our specs, but that is very cumbersome and puts low-level implementation details into all parts of our tests, which will make refactoring harder. So here's what we've added to our spec:

```
subject(:todo_list) { Todo::TodoList.new(::REDIS_CLIENT) }
let(:todos) do
  [
    {
      'text' => 'Water the garden',
      'done' => false
    },
    {
      'text' => 'Get some sleep',
      'done' => false
    }
  ]
end
context '#add' do
  it 'stores the todo in redis' do
    raw_list = ::REDIS_CLIENT.lrange(described_class::LIST_NAME, 0, -1)
```

```
        expect(raw_list.size).to eq(0)

        todo_list.add(todos.first['text'])

        raw_list = ::REDIS_CLIENT.lrange(described_class::LIST_NAME, 0,
    -1)

        expect(raw_list.size).to eq(1)

        actual   = MultiJson.decode(raw_list.first)
        expected = todos.first
        expect(actual).to eq(expected)
    end

    it 'returns all todos' do
        raw_list = ::REDIS_CLIENT.lrange(described_class::LIST_NAME, 0,
    -1)

        expect(raw_list.size).to eq(0)

        todo_list.add(todos[1]['text'])
        actual = todo_list.add(todos[0]['text'])

        expect(actual).to eq(todos)
    end
  end
end
```

We're assuming that the todos will be stored in a Redis list, which we access with the `lrange` method. There are other possible implementations, such as using a hash or zset, but a list is good enough. We could also have used mocks in our tests to check that the appropriate calls to Redis were made instead of actually using it. That's a judgment call. In this case, this code is not doing much if we mock the calls to Redis, so it's better to just write to Redis. Remember that we've already configured our specs to flush our Redis after each example, so we don't have to worry about any stored values persisting between tests.

The examples are very simple. In the first one, we check that the Redis list is empty, then add a todo to it and then check that the list now has the todo. The second example is similar except that this time we check for the return value of the add method. If we run these specs now, we'll get an error message that includes `undefined method `add'`. Let's create that method now in `lib/todo_list.rb`:

```
    LIST_NAME='re:08:todo_list'
    def add(text)
      new_todo = {
        'text' => text,
```

```
        'done' => false
    }

    @redis_client.lpush(LIST_NAME,MultiJson.encode(new_todo))

    @redis_client.lrange(LIST_NAME, 0, -1).map do |s|
      MultiJson.decode(s)
    end
  end
end
```

It's very simple. We use re:08 as a namespace for our list's key (re from the initials of this book's title and 08 from the chapter number) and use Redis's lpush method to add a JSON-encoded todo object to it. Then we read back the entire list of todo objects and return them, parsed as JSON.

If we run our specs now, they will all pass. Let's quickly move to define more of our tests. Here are the specs for all and delete_all:

```
context '#all' do
  it 'returns all todos' do
    expect(todo_list.all).to eq([])

    todo_list.add(todos[1]['text'])
    todo_list.add(todos[0]['text'])

    expect(todo_list.all).to eq(todos)
  end
end

context '#delete_all' do
  it 'deletes all todos and returns an empty array' do
    expect(todo_list.all).to eq([])

    todo_list.add(todos[1]['text'])
    todo_list.add(todos[0]['text'])

    expect(todo_list.all).to eq(todos)

    actual = todo_list.delete_all
    expect(todo_list.all).to eq([])
    expect(actual).to eq([])
  end
end
```

We run our specs, watch them fail, and then create the method definitions, which are quite simple:

```
def all
  @redis_client.lrange(LIST_NAME, 0, -1).map do |s|
    MultiJson.decode(s)
  end
end

def delete_all
  @redis_client.del(LIST_NAME)
  self.all
end
```

Now, when we move on to `delete_finished`, we'll notice a big problem. We have no way of marking a `todo` item as finished. It's not hard to add such a method to `Todo::TodoList`, but now that we think about it, we notice that we didn't even have such a method in our AngularJS service. We totally overlooked this implementation. Our view does update the JavaScript model when we check off an item, but that never makes it to our API backend so it won't ever be stored. We'll also need a way to switch a finished item back to unfinished.

So now we have to define a `Todo::TodoList.toggle_done` method, then implement an API endpoint to toggle a `todo` object's `done` property back and forth. But how can we identify which `todo` to update? Our todos have a text field, but there could be multiple fields with the same text. Let's add a unique ID to each `todo` item to allow us to find them. The Redis list structure doesn't allow an ID field to be set or queried, so that choice doesn't seem that great now. Let's switch to using a Redis hash instead, which will more easily accommodate an ID field. However, we lose the order of our `todo` list with a hash, which does not preserve any order. We'll compensate for that with a little trick of our own, adding a timestamp field to each `todo` item, which we can then use to sort the list once we retrieve it from Redis.

There are going to be a lot of changes, and there will be a natural process of trial and error. We'll go back and forth between the `Todo::TodoList` code and the specs until we get something that works. At the end of the process, we will have this in `spec/lib/todo_list_spec.rb`:

```
require_relative '../spec_helper'
require_relative '../../lib/todo_list'

RSpec.describe Todo::TodoList, redis: true do
  subject(:todo_list) { Todo::TodoList.new(::REDIS_CLIENT) }
  let(:todos) do
    [
```

```ruby
        {
          'text' => 'Water the garden',
          'done' => false
        },
        {
          'text' => 'Get some sleep',
          'done' => false
        }
      ]
    end

    def todos_with_ids(ids)
      todos.each_with_index.map do |hsh, i|
        hsh['id'] = ids[i]
        hsh
      end
    end

    def get_raw_hash
      ::REDIS_CLIENT.hgetall(described_class::HASH_NAME)
    end

    context '.new' do
      it 'expects a Redis client' do
        expect{
          described_class.new(:foo)
        }.to raise_error('Expected a Redis instance, got Symbol')
      end

      it 'sets @redis_client' do
        tl = described_class.new(::REDIS_CLIENT)

        actual = tl.instance_variable_get(:@redis_client)

        expect(actual).to eq(::REDIS_CLIENT)
      end
    end

    context '#add' do
      it 'stores the todo in redis' do
        expect(get_raw_hash.size).to eq(0)

        todo_list.add(todos.first['text'])
```

```
    raw_hash = get_raw_hash
    expect(raw_hash.size).to eq(1)

    actual   = MultiJson.decode(raw_hash.values.first)
    expected = todos.first

    expect(actual['text']).to eq(expected['text'])
  end

  it 'returns the ID of added todo' do
    expect(get_raw_hash.size).to eq(0)

    id1 = todo_list.add(todos[0]['text'])
    id2 = todo_list.add(todos[1]['text'])

    expected1 = MultiJson.decode(get_raw_hash[id1])
    expected2 = MultiJson.decode(get_raw_hash[id2])

    expected1.delete('id')
    expected1.delete('ts')
    expected2.delete('id')
    expected2.delete('ts')

    expect(expected1).to eq(todos[0])
    expect(expected2).to eq(todos[1])
  end
end

context '#all' do
  it 'returns all todos' do
    expect(todo_list.all).to eq([])

    id1 = todo_list.add(todos[0]['text'])
    id2 = todo_list.add(todos[1]['text'])

    actual   = todo_list.all
    expected = todos_with_ids([id1, id2])
    expect(actual).to eq(expected)
  end
end

context '#delete_all' do
  it 'deletes all todos and returns an empty array' do
    expect(todo_list.all).to eq([])
```

```ruby
      id1 = todo_list.add(todos[0]['text'])
      id2 = todo_list.add(todos[1]['text'])

      all_todos = todos_with_ids([id1, id2])
      expect(todo_list.all).to eq(all_todos)

      actual = todo_list.delete_all
      expect(todo_list.all).to eq([])
      expect(actual).to eq([])
    end
  end

  context '#toggle_done' do
    it 'updates an item as done by ID and returns the updated item' do
      todo_list.add(todos[0]['text'])
      id = todo_list.add(todos[1]['text'])

      actual = todo_list.toggle_done(id)

      expect(actual['text']).to eq(todos.last['text'])
      expect(actual['done']).to eq(true)

      expect(todo_list.all.last['done']).to eq(true)
    end
  end

  context '.delete_finished' do
    let(:finished_todos) do
      [
        {
          'text' => 'Buy cheese',
          'done' => true
        },
        {
          'text' => 'Fix the computer',
          'done' => true
        }
      ]
    end
    it 'deletes finished todos and returns all remaining todos' do
      id1 = todo_list.add(todos[0]['text'])
      id2 = todo_list.add(todos[1]['text'])
      id3 = todo_list.add(finished_todos[0]['text'])
      id4 = todo_list.add(finished_todos[1]['text'])
```

```
        todo_list.toggle_done(id3)
        todo_list.toggle_done(id4)

        actual   = todo_list.delete_finished
        expected = todos_with_ids([id1, id2])

        expect(actual).to eq(expected)
        expect(todo_list.all).to eq(expected)
      end
    end
end
```

That's long. Take some time to look over it. You'll notice things have changed throughout. We've changed the return value of the add method to return the ID, which we then can use for other things.

After you've understood the specs, let's look at `lib/todo_list.rb` in its final form:

```
require 'redis'
require 'multi_json'
require 'securerandom'

module Todo
end

class Todo::TodoList
  HASH_NAME='re:08:todo_list'

  def initialize(redis_client)
    if ! (redis_client.is_a?(Redis))
      raise "Expected a Redis instance, got #{redis_client.class}"
    end

    @redis_client = redis_client
  end

  def add(text)
    id       = SecureRandom.uuid
    new_todo = {
      'id'   => id,
      'text' => text,
      'done' => false,
      'ts'   => Time.now.to_f.to_s
    }
```

```
      @redis_client.hset(HASH_NAME, id, MultiJson.encode(new_todo))

    id
  end

  def all
    @redis_client.hgetall(HASH_NAME).values.map do |s|
      MultiJson.decode(s)
    end.sort_by do |hsh|
      hsh['ts']
    end.map do |hsh|
      hsh.delete('ts')
      hsh
    end
  end

  def delete_all
    @redis_client.del(HASH_NAME)
    self.all
  end

  def toggle_done(id)
    old_val = @redis_client.hget(HASH_NAME, id)

    if (old_val)
      new_val = MultiJson.decode(old_val)
      new_val['done'] = ! new_val['done']
      @redis_client.hset(HASH_NAME, id, MultiJson.encode(new_val))
      new_val
    end
  end

  def delete_finished
    self.all.select do |hsh|
      if hsh['done']
        @redis_client.hdel(HASH_NAME, hsh['id'])
        false
      else
        true
      end
    end
  end
end
```

We're using the standard Ruby `SecureRandom` library to generate unique IDs every time we add an item. We're also setting a very accurate timestamp for each item and we use it for sorting. Note that the timestamp is a purely internal value that we don't expose to users of `Todo::TodoList`.

Now what? We go back to our API specs and finish them up. Let's remember to add an endpoint to handle marking an item as done (or not done). Here's `spec/api/todo_api_spec.rb` now:

```ruby
require_relative '../api_helper'

RSpec.describe Todo::API, api: true, redis: true do
  # create a new browser session before each example
  let!(:browser) { RackTestBrowser.new_browser }

  def parsed_todos
    MultiJson.decode(browser.last_response.body)['todos']
  end

  context 'GET /api/v1/todos' do
    it 'returns an empty array at first' do
      browser.get '/api/v1/todos'

      expect(browser.last_response.status).to eq(200)
      expect(parsed_todos).to eq([])

      browser.post '/api/v1/todos', {'text' => 'my first todo'}
      browser.post '/api/v1/todos', {'text' => 'my second todo'}

      browser.get '/api/v1/todos'

      expect(browser.last_response.status).to eq(200)
      expect(parsed_todos.size).to eq(2)
      expect(parsed_todos[0]['text']).to eq('my first todo')
      expect(parsed_todos[1]['text']).to eq('my second todo')
    end
  end

  context 'POST /api/v1/todos' do
    it 'creates a new todo' do
      browser.post '/api/v1/todos', {'text' => 'my first todo'}
      expect(browser.last_response.status).to eq(201)
      expect(parsed_todos.size).to eq(1)
      expect(parsed_todos[0]['text']).to eq('my first todo')
```

```
      end
    end

    context 'DELETE /api/v1/todos' do
      it 'delete all todos' do
        browser.post '/api/v1/todos', {'text' => 'my first todo'}
        browser.post '/api/v1/todos', {'text' => 'my second todo'}

        browser.get '/api/v1/todos'

        expect(browser.last_response.status).to eq(200)
        expect(parsed_todos.size).to eq(2)

        browser.delete 'api/v1/todos'
        expect(browser.last_response.status).to eq(200)
        expect(parsed_todos).to eq([])
      end
    end

    context 'POST /api/v1/todos/:id/toggle_done' do
      it 'marks the todo as done' do
        browser.post '/api/v1/todos', {'text' => 'my first todo'}
        browser.post '/api/v1/todos', {'text' => 'my second todo'}

        browser.get '/api/v1/todos'

        expect(browser.last_response.status).to eq(200)
        expect(parsed_todos.size).to eq(2)
        expect(parsed_todos[0]['done']).to eq(false)

        id = parsed_todos[0]['id']

        browser.post "api/v1/todos/#{id}/toggle_done", ""
        expect(browser.last_response.status).to eq(200)
        expect(parsed_todos.size).to eq(2)
        expect(parsed_todos[0]['done']).to eq(true)
      end
    end

    context 'DELETE /api/v1/todos/done' do
      it 'deletes all items marked as done' do
        browser.post '/api/v1/todos', {'text' => 'my first todo'}
        browser.post '/api/v1/todos', {'text' => 'my second todo'}
```

```
    browser.get '/api/v1/todos'

    expect(browser.last_response.status).to eq(200)
    id = parsed_todos[0]['id']

    browser.post "api/v1/todos/#{id}/toggle_done", ""

    browser.delete "api/v1/todos/done"
    expect(browser.last_response.status).to eq(200)
    expect(parsed_todos.size).to eq(1)
    expect(parsed_todos[0]['text']).to eq('my second todo')
  end
 end
end
```

We've also updated our `spec/api_helper.rb` file to pull in `spec/spec_helper.rb` in order to handle Redis flushing properly. I won't go into detail on these specs. They are pretty self-explanatory and most of the changes and additions are related to how we return data. Note that we are always returning a JSON object from our HTTP endpoints and not an array. This addresses a security vulnerability in JavaScript arrays and also makes for a more consistent format for results. If we run these API specs, they will all fail, since we need to adjust our API code. Take some time to look through the specs, run them, and understand them.

After you've familiarized yourself with the API specs, we can move on to look at the API implementation in `app.rb`:

```ruby
require 'sinatra/base'
require 'multi_json'

require_relative 'initializers/redis'
require_relative 'lib/todo_list'

module Todo
end

class Todo::API < Sinatra::Base
  helpers do
    def todo_list
      @todo_list = Todo::TodoList.new(::REDIS_CLIENT)
    end
  end

  get '/api/v1/todos' do
```

```
      todos = todo_list.all
      MultiJson.encode({'todos' => todos})
    end

    post '/api/v1/todos' do
      todo_list.add(params['text'])
      todos = todo_list.all

      status 201
      MultiJson.encode({'todos' => todos})
    end

    post '/api/v1/todos/:id/toggle_done' do
      todo_list.mark_done(params['id'])
      todos = todo_list.all

      status 200
      MultiJson.encode({'todos' => todos})
    end

    delete '/api/v1/todos' do
      todos = todo_list.delete_all
      MultiJson.encode({'todos' => todos})
    end

    delete '/api/v1/todos/done' do
      todos = todo_list.delete_finished
      MultiJson.encode({'todos' => todos})
    end
end
```

Step 3 – finishing the view

It's been a long chapter, but we are almost done! We now need to incorporate this API into our AngularJS controller and service. Actually, we only need a small addition to the service, a small change to the controller, and no changes at all to the view.

First, in our service `static/js/todo_list.js`, we'll need to add a method to handle `toggleDone`:

```
'use strict';

// define the model to handle the data
var TodoList = function ($http) {
  // ... same as before ...

  // the new method
  store.toggleDone = function(id) {
    return $http.post('/api/v1/todos/' + id + '/toggle_done').
then(returnTodos);
  }

  return store;
};
```

In `static/js/todo_list_controller.js`, we'll change the `$scope.toggleDone` method to use this new `TodoList.toggleDone` method:

```
$scope.toggleDone = function(todo) {
  TodoList.toggleDone(todo.id).then(function(todos){
    $scope.todos = todos;
  });
}
```

That's it! We're ready for the grand finale. Let's run all of our specs and features at once:

```
Terminal
$ APP_HOST=local rspec spec/**/*_feature.rb spec/**/*_spec.rb —format documenta
tion
Booting a local server using config.ru...

Todo::API
  GET /api/v1/todos
    returns an empty array at first
  POST /api/v1/todos
    creates a new todo
  DELETE /api/v1/todos
    delete all todos
  POST /api/v1/todos/:id/toggle_done
    marks the todo as done
  DELETE /api/v1/todos/done
    marks the todo as done

Manage to-do items
  add
  mark as done

Todo::TodoList
  .new
    expects a Redis client
    sets @redis_client
  #add
    stores the todo in redis
    returns the ID of added todo
  #all
    returns all todos
  #delete_all
    deletes all todos and returns an empty array
  #toggle_done
    updates an item as done by ID and returns the updated item
  .delete_finished
    deletes finished todos and returns all remaining todos

Finished in 7.11 seconds (files took 0.73029 seconds to load)
15 examples, 0 failures

$
```

It all works. Was all the effort worth it? Think about it a bit and we'll come back to discuss the pros and cons of BDD.

There's another very interesting trick we can pull off. Let's try to run our feature file against the public `todomvc.com` website's implementation of a todo list manager. Although the implementation is totally different, the features we are testing for should be the same.

Here's what happens:

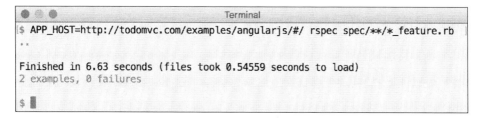

Both features pass. You should see your browser open up with the very stylish TodoMVC version of the todo list:

This neat trick was made possible by the fact that our features and markup were tailored to match that of the `todomvc.com` version of the site. But it shows a very interesting high-level use for feature files. We can totally reimplement an app and test its features very easily. Also, being able to target any URL with our features is very useful for testing out QA or staging servers running various versions of our code. We can easily integrate such feature tests with a continuous integration system such as **Travis CI** or **Jenkins** to make sure our overall features are working throughout the development and deployment process. This is very important, as realistic development will involve locally running sites, QA and staging servers, and even production systems. We can target anything and our specs will work the same way, since we've decided to use outside-in, black-box specs that do not assume any control of the running application from within the specs. This also explains why we set `Capybara.run_server` to `false`, since our specs do not start the servers we are going to hit.

Another important detail is the `before` hook that resets the page. Since we are using a black-box approach, we can't just wipe out a database to reset the state of the application. That means all of our actions will persist from one scenario to the next. In order to start from a clean slate, we're marking all items as completed and then clearing them. That is pretty easy, given the simplicity of the todo list manager app. However, for more complex apps with more stateful interactions, it may be very tricky to reset to a clean state. Managing state for specs is the greatest challenge for black-box testing. Often, you will need to create accounts or use an admin interface to manage state. You can also cheat a bit and use direct database queries or other non-black-box means to reset state. There are trade-offs in each scenario, but one benefit of sticking to the black-box approach is that you know you have full administrative capabilities in the app, since your specs require them just to run. You also get some testing of these administrative functions out of your specs.

The pros and cons of BDD

This chapter has been very long. We've written tests at multiple levels, from the high-level black-box feature (which isn't a test, strictly speaking) to the functional API specs, to the model-level specs for `Todo::TodoList`. We could also have written functional and unit tests for our AngularJS code. Is this worth it? When does all this testing become too much?

The answer is not easy and will depend on the system under consideration. The benefits of BDD are the rigor and modularity that come from so many levels of specifications. However, there is a cost and the specs can start to get in the way. Also, as these specs grow in number, they can become difficult to maintain and actually start hindering efforts to change the code. This usually happens because not much time and effort are dedicated to the test code itself.

In my opinion, BDD is a valuable approach to software engineering but it isn't appropriate for most situations. Still, taking the outside-in approach can be refreshing and open up valuable new insights into what really matters in your app. But it isn't practical to do everything with BDD or using the outside-in approach.

A professional software engineer spends much more time maintaining and changing existing code than they do creating brand new apps from scratch. For those common coding tasks, such as fixing bugs or adding new features, if no BDD feature is defined, it can be too burdensome to create it. If there are BDD features defined, it may be a burden to modify them. Having worked with gigantic code bases full of feature files, I can testify to the huge costs that can be associated with taking BDD too far.

However, measured use of BDD can help an engineer to make big improvements to a system by redefining the very feature itself and seeing the big picture. The trick is to use BDD when there is potential for something fundamental to change. Also, it is imperative to write the bare minimum of code for feature files. These are slow, complex, and prone to brittleness. Quality is king for feature files, even more so than normal specs, and the quantity must be minimized.

Simple Rack authentication middleware

Now that we've built an API, we can start thinking about securing it. Both for the users of our web UI and other users that directly hit the API from other sites, authentication is a critical feature that we're missing. We won't build a complete authentication solution, but we'll add the critical authentication middleware that will be the main component in an authentication system. We'll see that it won't be much more work.

We briefly mentioned Rack middleware in *Chapter 7, Building an App from the Outside In with Behavior-Driven Development*, when we used `Rack::Static` to serve static assets. Now we're going to add middleware that will authenticate every request before it hits our app.

First, let's start with a simple example with a file called `auth_middleware.rb`:

```
class AuthMiddleware
  def initialize(app, opts={})
    if ! opts[:secret].is_a?(String)
      raise ':secret is required'
    end

    @app    = app
    @secret = opts[:secret]
  end
```

```
      def call(env)
        if env['HTTP_AUTHORIZATION'] == @secret
          @app.call(env)
        else
          [
            401,
            {},
            ['Not authorized']
          ]
        end
      end
    end
```

And here is what we have in `config.ru`:

```
require 'rack'
require_relative 'tiny_rack_app'
require_relative 'auth_middleware'

app_with_auth = Rack::Builder.new do
  if ! ENV['TINY_SECRET'].is_a?(String)
    abort 'TINY_SECRET env var must be set'
  end

  use AuthMiddleware, secret: ENV['TINY_SECRET']
  run TinyRackApp.new
end


run app_with_auth
```

Let's see this in action before diving into the explanation of the code. We'll use Rack's `rackup` command to start the app:

```
$ rackup
TINY_SECRET env var must be set
$ TINY_SECRET=banana rackup config.ru
[2015-12-07 23:20:12] INFO  WEBrick 1.3.1
[2015-12-07 23:20:12] INFO  ruby 2.2.0 (2014-12-25) [x86_64-darwin14]
[2015-12-07 23:20:12] INFO  WEBrick::HTTPServer#start: pid=23905
port=9292
```

Note that we set the password to `banana` using the `TINY_SECRET` environment variable. Now we'll make two requests to the server (note that it is running on `port 9292` this time, which is the default when using `rackup`):

```
$ curl --verbose http://localhost:9292
* Rebuilt URL to: http://localhost:9292/
*   Trying ::1...
* Connected to localhost (::1) port 9292 (#0)
> GET / HTTP/1.1
> Host: localhost:9292
> User-Agent: curl/7.43.0
> Accept: */*
>
< HTTP/1.1 401 Unauthorized
< Transfer-Encoding: chunked
< Server: WEBrick/1.3.1 (Ruby/2.2.0/2014-12-25)
< Date: Tue, 08 Dec 2015 07:21:41 GMT
< Connection: Keep-Alive
<
* Connection #0 to host localhost left intact
Not authorized
$ curl --verbose http://localhost:9292 --header 'Authorization:
banana'
* Rebuilt URL to: http://localhost:9292/
*   Trying ::1...
* Connected to localhost (::1) port 9292 (#0)
> GET / HTTP/1.1
> Host: localhost:9292
> User-Agent: curl/7.43.0
> Accept: */*
> Authorization: banana
>
< HTTP/1.1 200 OK
< Content-Type: text/plain
< Transfer-Encoding: chunked
< Server: WEBrick/1.3.1 (Ruby/2.2.0/2014-12-25)
< Date: Tue, 08 Dec 2015 07:21:55 GMT
< Connection: Keep-Alive
<
* Connection #0 to host localhost left intact
Hello, World!
```

The first request gave us a `401` HTTP status code and a `Not authorized` body. In the second request, we supplied an HTTP request header with the password `banana` and got a `200` status with our app's `Hello, World!` message. The first request never even reached our `TinyRackApp` code because the middleware responded. The second request was passed through the middleware and reached `TinyRackApp`.

JSON Web Token

Using plain-text passwords such as `banana` is not at all secure. We should use a token scheme to make our authentication secure. We'll use the **JSON Web Token (JWT)** standard (defined in RFC 7519: `https://tools.ietf.org/html/rfc7519`), which is very simple but also very powerful. JWT allows the client to use a shared secret (such as `banana`) to sign a set of claims to generate a token which is then sent to the server. A claim is a piece of information that the client sends to the server and which must be authenticated. Most commonly, this would be the username but it can include any set of data. Previous to JWT, such info was included in various ways and there was room for error due to poorly designed claims encoding or mistaken implementations. Many different kinds of digest algorithms are supported, as well as asymmetric public/ private key pairs to generate the token from the claims. This allows for the security mechanism to be easily adjusted without having to change the overall authentication scheme. Finally, JWT includes built-in support for the expiration of tokens, which is a very important security feature to prevent reuse of tokens.

In order to use JWT in Ruby, we'll use the `ruby-jwt` gem. It's not hard to write the code to implement JWT ourselves, and it's a very good exercise, but it's a good idea to use standard tools for security unless we're willing to become experts, since there are many subtle considerations that must be taken into account to ensure security. All we need from the `ruby-jwt` gem are two simple methods: `JWT.encode` to create a token, and `JWT.decode` to process a token.

Without further ado, here is our JWT authentication middleware:

```
require 'jwt'

class JWTAuthMiddleware
  def initialize(app, opts={})
    if ! opts[:secret].is_a?(String)
      raise ":secret is a required option"
    end
```

```ruby
    @app    = app
    @secret = opts[:secret]
  end

  def call(env)
    auth_header = env['HTTP_AUTHORIZATION']

    if ! auth_header.is_a?(String)
      raise "No auth header detected"
    end

    # header looks like: Authorization: Bearer
eyJ0eXAiOiJKV1QiLCJhbGciOiJIUzI1NiJ9.eyJ1c2VyIjoiYm9iIn0.
sKtaCUiPRq3OWHPN6FNqC6ajyXKGGf92f_Ng488RSJc
    token = auth_header.gsub(/^Bearer /, '')

    # raises an error if token is invalid
    payload = JWT.decode(token, @secret)

    env['rack.jwt.payload'] = payload

    @app.call(env)
  rescue
    puts $!.inspect

    [
      401,
      {},
      ["Authorization failed"]
    ]
  end
end
```

To use this middleware in our Rack app, we would simply add a few lines to `config.ru` to load it before we run our main app:

```ruby
require_relative 'jwt_auth_middleware'

secret = ENV['JWT_SECRET'] || 'completely_insecure'
use JWTAuthMiddleware, secret: secret
```

I'll leave the task of incorporating JWT authentication into the feature files, specs, and views as an exercise. It will be a bit of a challenge, as testing authentication in feature files is not easy, but with all the work we've done together, I'm sure you'll be able to tackle this challenge.

Summary

In this chapter, we created a simple `todo` list manager web app following the full BDD process, and covered some of the important details for managing this outside-in, black-box approach to features. We learned how to incorporate TDD into the BDD process to create functional and unit tests for the lower-level components of our systems. We saw how we can run our features against external sites and discussed the pros and cons of BDD. Finally, we learned about adding authentication using Rack middleware while leaving the full implementation as an exercise for the motivated reader.

9
Configurability

In this chapter, we will learn how to configure applications using simple, robust tools based on environment variables. We'll learn about configurability and its importance to testability. We'll deal with real-world configuration concerns that come up during development and testing. We'll address these concerns in a way that makes testing easy but addresses the safety and security requirements of a production environment.

Although we won't directly use RSpec at all in this chapter, its contents are the most important in this book. That is because proper configuration management is fundamental to testability and is something that is often done wrong. You can learn about RSpec easily from other sources, but configurability is one of those real-world concerns that is difficult to learn except the hard way: though direct experience, making mistakes, and learning from them through trial and error.

Here is what we will cover in this chapter:

- Configuration via environment variables
- Loading environment variables from a file
- Overriding configurations for testing
- Making configurations easily accessible for inspection
- Managing sensitive configuration values
- Ensuring required configurations are set at start time

Configuration and testability

In our test and application code throughout this book, we've seen many examples of configurations set by environment variables. Here are some examples to refresh our memory:

- In *Chapter 3, Taking Control of State with Doubles and Hooks* and *Chapter 5, Simulating External Services*, Redis was configured using `ENV['WQ_REDIS_URL']`

- In *Chapter 5, Simulating External Services*, network connectivity in specs was set with `ENV['ALLOW_NET_CONNECT']`

- In *Chapter 6, Driving a Web Browser with Capybara* and *Chapter 7, Building an App from the Outside In with Behavior-Driven Development*, the browser used to run e2e tests with Capybara was set with `ENV['BROWSER']`

- In *Chapter 8, Tackling the Challenges of End-to-end Testing*, the Sinatra environments and authentication secret were set using `ENV['SINATRA_ENV']` and `ENV['JWT_SECRET']`

Using environment variables in this way gave us powerful options when running our app and its tests while maintaining a clean separation between code, tests, and configuration. Environment variables are a commonly used mechanism to configure applications. They are simple, portable, and flexible.

What is so important about configuration?

It turns out that real-world apps require a high degree of configurability to be practical. During development, testing, and deployments to various types of environment, the app must be configured slightly differently. We simply can't develop our app or run tests without some ability to configure certain features.

Once we have a number of different configuration options, the danger arises of confusion and misconfiguration. We may forget to set an important configuration that is required for correct functioning, for example, a database URL configuration, without which the application cannot even start. We may have default values that are dangerous when used in certain environments. For example, if the default value for the database connection URL was our production server, we may wipe out all of our app's data in the production environment by running our local unit tests.

What does all this have to do with testing?

A reliable set of tests is impossible without a high level of configurability in code and tests. Tests will fail apparently randomly on different systems due to hidden dependencies on configurations that may only work on certain machines or on certain networks. Tests will pass although the code is not working properly due to misconfiguration. Worst of all, these types of issues are very difficult to detect, diagnose, and fix. A system with bad configurability is very hard to fix, as code that has not been cleanly separated from configuration will require basic rewrites to become configurable. Such basic rewrites are costly and inevitably introduce bugs. Therefore, we have to consider configurability from the beginning if we are to achieve testability.

All of the examples we've worked with have had a decent amount of configurability, although the subject has not been a primary focus until now. However, we can do much better. To address the need for configuration that is flexible and manageable, we'll need to put some effort into the configuration system. One important consideration is to keep configuration minimal. Too many configuration options, with some interacting together, will lead to confusion, regardless of how many tools we build to manage them.

Environment variables allow us to set simple string variables when we start a process. We can change a configuration simply by changing the command used to start the process. We've seen many examples of this throughout the book. For example, we could run our specs with the Firefox browser using `BROWSER=firefox rspec` and with the Chrome browser using `BROWSER=chrome rspec`. Within our Ruby code, we can look up the value of the configuration by accessing the Hash-like `ENV` global variable, for example, `ENV['BROWSER']`.

As our application grows, so will the number of configurations. Specifying each of these on the command line will be burdensome and prone to error. We'll need to organize our configurations somehow. There are many approaches to this, some of which are quite sophisticated. We'll learn about a simple, file-based approach, which can be used on its own just fine in large, real-world apps, or combined with more complex tools as well.

File-based configuration management

What we're going to do is to put all of our configurations into a file and load them from the file when we start our app. This is quite simple to get started with, but we'll have to evolve in order to support some important basic needs. We'll start with a config file, which we'll name `.env`, which is a commonly used convention, although the name is actually not important. Here are the contents of the file:

```
TODO_STORE='redis'
REDIS_URL='redis://127.0.0.1:6379/0'
REDIS_PASSWORD='cantguessthis'
```

The format is that of variable declarations in a Bash shell script. This is appropriate because using environment variables will force us to use Bash variables in the end. We avoid the confusion of type conversions by declaring the variables in the same way. Had we used JSON or another more powerful format, we would have to contend with conversion of types for integers, arrays, and other non-String types allowed by the format.

The next step is to load these variables into the environment. Let's do some experiments on the command line to see how we can get these environment variables set:

```
Terminal
$ echo $TODO_STORE $REDIS_URL $REDIS_PASSWORD

$ cat .env
TODO_STORE='redis'
REDIS_URL='redis://127.0.0.1:6379/0'
REDIS_PASSWORD='cantguessthis'
$ cat .env | xargs
TODO_STORE=redis REDIS_URL=redis://127.0.0.1:6379/0 REDIS_PASSWORD=cantguessthis
$ (export $(cat .env| xargs) && echo $TODO_STORE $REDIS_URL $REDIS_PASSWORD)
redis redis://127.0.0.1:6379/0 cantguessthis
$ echo $TODO_STORE $REDIS_URL $REDIS_PASSWORD
```

By using a combination of the common Unix tools export, cat, and xargs, we can load the environment variables in our .env file for any command. To learn more about each of these commands, please refer to their man pages (e.g. man cat on the command line) or other documentation, widely available online.

The final template is:

```
$ (export $(cat .env| xargs) && <anycommand>)
```

We note that the environment variables were only loaded for the command we ran and did not persist afterwards. This is important as we could pollute our environment during development by changing the environment in our shell. A polluted environment can lead to false positives, false negatives, and a lot of frustration.

Let's use this method to run a little Ruby script to demonstrate how the environment variables make their way from the `.env` file into Ruby. We'll use a dummy Ruby script called `app.rb`:

```ruby
require 'pp'

config = {
  'TODO_STORE'     => ENV['TODO_STORE'],
  'REDIS_URL'      => ENV['REDIS_URL'],
  'REDIS_PASSWORD' => ENV['REDIS_PASSWORD']
}

pp config

puts
puts "App would start here..."

exit 0
```

When we run it with our template, here's what we'll see:

```
● ● ●                              Terminal
$ (export $(cat .env| xargs) && ruby app.rb)
{"TODO_STORE"=>"redis",
 "REDIS_URL"=>"redis://127.0.0.1:6379/0",
 "REDIS_PASSWORD"=>"cantguessthis"}

App would start here...
```

There isn't much to this. We take note that we just used a local variable named `config` to store our configs. This isn't going to work for a real app. We'll need to store these configs in a more durable location, like a constant or global variable. Also note that if we were missing some of these configs, nothing would happen. Let's try changing our `config` file to remove two of the configs and see what we get:

```
● ● ●                              Terminal
$ echo "TODO_STORE='redis'" > .env
$ cat .env
TODO_STORE='redis'
$ (export $(cat .env| xargs) && ruby app.rb)
{"TODO_STORE"=>"redis", "REDIS_URL"=>nil, "REDIS_PASSWORD"=>nil}

App would start here...
$
```

The configs are `nil`. This could lead to errors or a total crash some time later in the program. It would be great to specify required configurations and crash on startup if any are missing. We'll also need an easy way to distinguish our app's environment variables from those that have nothing to do with it. It's easy to have a slight typo in our code and not pick up an important environment variable. If we had a naming convention for our environment variables, we could detect them all automatically and guard against accidental collisions with generic environment variables (for example, `$PATH`).

Another issue is how to override a specific configuration. This is very useful for development and testing. It should be easy to set an environment variable when running a command, but our template is a little complex and adding environment variable declarations to it is not very elegant:

```
                                Terminal
$ (export $(cat .env| xargs) && ruby app.rb)
{"TODO_STORE"=>"redis", "REDIS_URL"=>nil, "REDIS_PASSWORD"=>nil}

App would start here...
$ (export $(cat .env| xargs) && REDIS_URL=foo REDIS_PASSWORD=bar ruby app.rb)
{"TODO_STORE"=>"redis", "REDIS_URL"=>"foo", "REDIS_PASSWORD"=>"bar"}

App would start here...
$
```

This hurts the eyes and will lead to confusion as we add more configurations. It would be very nice to have a simpler command to start our app. Then, declaring environment variables wouldn't be a big deal. What would be nice is a simple `start.sh` command, which would allow us to set the environment variables like this:

```
$ REDIS_URL=foo REDIS_PASSWORD=bar ./start.sh
```

There is another concern. What about badly formatted lines in the config file? What if there was a missing quote? Or if a line wasn't at all formatted like a key-value pair as we expect? It would be very helpful to quickly detect malformed lines and raise a clear error on startup.

Finally, our config file format doesn't explicitly handle blank lines or comments. We can get away with some cases by accident, but many common cases will not work as expected. For example, try commenting out every line in the config file and see what happens when we run our start command:

```
●  ●  ●                          Terminal
$ cat .env
# TODO_STORE='redis'
# REDIS_URL='redis://127.0.0.1:6379/0'
# REDIS_PASSWORD='cantguessthis'
$ echo $TODO_STORE $REDIS_URL $REDIS_PASSWORD

$ (export $(cat .env| xargs) && ruby app.rb)
{"TODO_STORE"=>"redis",
 "REDIS_URL"=>"redis://127.0.0.1:6379/0",
 "REDIS_PASSWORD"=>"cantguessthis"}

App would start here...
$ ▊
```

This isn't what we expected. In order to have clean, maintainable configs, it is a good idea to support blank lines and comments.

In the next section we'll look at a solution that addresses all these concerns.

A better configuration manager

First, we'll use a script that does one simple thing. It reads the config file, validates its format, and outputs its contents without any blank lines or comments. The script is significantly more complex than the little snippet we had before, although we're only adding a few modest features. This is a common pattern which should be carefully considered: adding a couple of small features results in a very large increase in complexity. In this case, the added complexity is justified, but we shouldn't make the decision lightly.

The script is called `env-echo.sh` and here is what it contains:

```
#!/usr/bin/env bash

# Echoes environment variables from a file
# -- ignores comment lines
# -- ignores blank lines
# -- validates format of each line to ensure a proper variable
declaration
# -- requires variable names to have a prefix to avoid collisions
# -- skips variables in file if already set, allowing overrides

# safety settings to ensure errors in this script are caught
set -o errexit
set -o pipefail
```

```
# set default prefix
: ${CONFIG_PREFIX:='RE09_'}

# if provided, use first argument as path to .env file
if [ ! -z "$1" ]
then
  readonly DOT_ENV_FILE="$1"

# set default path to config file
else
  # first, safely determine directory where this script is located
  DIR="$(cd "$(dirname "$0")" && pwd)"
  readonly DOT_ENV_FILE="$DIR/.env"
fi

# ensure .env file exists
if [ ! -f "${DOT_ENV_FILE}" ]
then
  echo "File not found: ${DOT_ENV_FILE}" 1>&2;
  exit 1
fi

# only allow alphanumeric and underscore for key names
readonly VALID_KEY_NAME_REGEX='[A-Za-z0-9_]+'

# force all values to be wrapped in single quotes
readonly VALID_VALUE_REGEX="'[^']+'"

readonly LINE_REGEX="^${VALID_KEY_NAME_REGEX}=${VALID_VALUE_REGEX}$"

while read -r line
do
  # validate basic NAME='VALUE' format
  if [[ ! "$line" =~ ${LINE_REGEX} ]]
  then
    echo "Badly formatted line:"
    echo
    echo "  $line"
    echo
    echo
    echo "* Variable name must include only alphanumeric characters or
underscore."
```

```
      echo "* Value must be enclosed in single quotes."
      exit 1
   fi

   # validate variable name starts with required prefix
   if [[ ! "$line" =~ ^${CONFIG_PREFIX} ]]
   then
      echo "Variable name does not start with correct prefix:"
      echo
      echo "  $line"
      echo
      echo
      echo "Try:"
      echo
      echo "  ${CONFIG_PREFIX}$line"
      exit 1
   fi

   # extracts key name by finding the first '=' character,
   # via bash parameter expansion:
   # https://www.gnu.org/software/bash/manual/html_node/Shell-
Parameter-Expansion.html
   key=${line%%=*}

   # check if variable named $key already defined
   if [ ${!key} ]
   then
      # env var already set, e.g. to override value in .env file
      # note the warning message is output to STDERR
      echo "skipping $key in file (already set to '${!key}')" 1>&2;
   else
      echo "${line}"
   fi

# remove comments then remove blank lines with grep
done < <(grep -v '^#' "${DOT_ENV_FILE}" | grep .)
```

The comments should explain how it functions. We won't go into the implementation details here. However, it is worth remarking that this is a Bash script and not Ruby code. This is an important point.

Bash is practically universally available and we rarely need to worry about having the proper version of Bash on any given system. Had we written this script in Ruby, we would have introduced a dependency that is not easily managed for this basic part of our system since Ruby is not universally available and we would likely require a specific version of Ruby. What makes this unacceptable for the configuration loading part of our code is that we are likely to rely on certain environment variables to properly load the proper version of Ruby (for example, using `rbenv`) and Ruby dependency management tools such as **Rubygems** and **Bundler**. It is a good practice to use universal tools, such as Bash, for very low-level concerns, such as loading configuration. Another advantage of Bash is that it makes it harder for us to introduce complexity via fancy features. With Ruby, we would be tempted to do much more since it would be easy.

Let's run the script with some input and see how it works. First we'll use a good config file:

```
$ cat .env
# ==================
# = CONFIGURATION =
# ==================

# allowed values are
#    * REDIS
#    * FILE
#    * HASH
RE09_TODO_STORE='REDIS'


# =======
# = URLs =
# =======

RE09_REDIS_PASSWORD='cantguessthis'


# =============
# = PASSWORDS =
# =============

RE09_REDIS_URL='redis://127.0.0.1:6379/0'
$ ./env-echo.sh
RE09_TODO_STORE='REDIS'
RE09_REDIS_PASSWORD='cantguessthis'
RE09_REDIS_URL='redis://127.0.0.1:6379/0'
$
```

It works as expected: all blank lines and comments are removed from the output. Now let's see what happens when we override a single config value:

```
● ● ●                         Terminal
$ RE09_TODO_STORE=something ./env-echo.sh
skipping RE09_TODO_STORE in file (already set to 'something')
RE09_REDIS_PASSWORD='cantguessthis'
RE09_REDIS_URL='redis://127.0.0.1:6379/0'
$ RE09_TODO_STORE=something ./env-echo.sh | xargs
skipping RE09_TODO_STORE in file (already set to 'something')
RE09_REDIS_PASSWORD=cantguessthis RE09_REDIS_URL=redis://127.0.0.1:6379/0
$ ▊
```

We see that we get a warning message telling us that the config was already set. This message is output to STDERR not STDOUT, which means the warning will not be included when we pipe the output, as we can see in the second command.

So far, so good. We also added some validation rules to the script to make sure there aren't any mistakes in the config file. Let's run the script against five bad config files and see what happens:

```
● ● ●                         Terminal
$ ./env-echo.sh .bad-env1
Variable name does not start with correct prefix:

    FOOBAR='123'


Try:

    RE09_FOOBAR='123'
$ ./env-echo.sh .bad-env2
Badly formatted line:

    j;alksjdl;kasj


* Variable name must include only alphanumeric characters or underscore.
* Value must be enclosed in single quotes.
$ ./env-echo.sh .bad-env3
Badly formatted line:

    WITH A SPACD ^$)* = foo


* Variable name must include only alphanumeric characters or underscore.
* Value must be enclosed in single quotes.
$ ./env-echo.sh .bad-env4
Badly formatted line:

    TODO_STORE="RE=DI=S"


* Variable name must include only alphanumeric characters or underscore.
* Value must be enclosed in single quotes.
$ ./env-echo.sh .bad-env5
Badly formatted line:

    RE09_FOOBAR=noquotes


* Variable name must include only alphanumeric characters or underscore.
* Value must be enclosed in single quotes.
$ ▊
```

We can see that we require a strict format of NAME='VALUE' and have some additional requirements for the variable name: it must be prefixed with RE09_ (taken from the title of this book and this chapter number) and it may contain only alphanumeric characters and underscores.

Now let's use the new script. We can modify our template to use the script instead of cat .env:

```
$ (export $(./env-echo.sh | xargs) && <anycommand>)
```

We can use this template with a slightly modified version of the dummy Ruby file app.rb that uses the "namespaced" environment variable names (for example, ENV['RE09_TODO_STORE'] instead of ENV['TODO_STORE']):

```
$ (export $(./env-echo.sh | xargs) && ruby app.rb)
{"RE09_TODO_STORE"=>"REDIS",
 "RE09_REDIS_URL"=>"redis://127.0.0.1:6379/0",
 "RE09_REDIS_PASSWORD"=>"cantguessthis"}

App would start here...
$
```

There are still a few improvements we can make. We'd like to enforce certain required configurations. And let's see how we can expose the loaded configs in an HTTP interface to help with monitoring and debugging. Let's also consider security considerations. We don't want to show any sensitive information stored in configurations, such as passwords. The safe approach to filtering information is to use a whitelist and mask all other values. Finally, instead of storing configs in ENV along with many other values, we would benefit from storing our configs in a dedicated constant. This will facilitate inspection and reduce the potential for confusion.

Putting all this together, we'll have a small web app that will show us the loaded configurations. This is similar to our dummy Ruby app, but it will serve as a realistic skeleton structure for a practical Rack web app.

The first file we'll need is a start script, which we'll call start.sh:

```
#!/usr/bin/env bash

set -o errexit
set -o pipefail
set -o nounset
```

```
DIR="$(cd "$(dirname "$0")" && pwd)"
export $($DIR/config/env-echo.sh | xargs)

# app-specific startup, in this case a Rack web app
rackup
```

This script assumes we've put our `.env` file in a folder named `config` then starts a rack app using the `rackup` command, which will load a file named `config.ru` in the same folder as `start.sh`.

Let's have a look at `config.ru` now:

```
require 'rack/builder'
require 'rack/parser'
require 'json'

require_relative('initializer')

map '/varz.json' do
  run TodoApp::CONFIG_RACK_APP
end
```

This file doesn't do much. It requires an initializer file called `initializer.rb` and then starts a simple Rack app with a single path at `/varz.json`, which simply returns the loaded configurations in JSON format. Here's what we have in `initializer.rb`, which ties everything together:

```
require_relative 'lib/config_loader'
require_relative 'lib/config_rack_app'

begin
  # find this app's config's, which all start with RE09_
  raw_configs = ENV.to_hash.select do |k, v|
    k =~ /^RE09_/
  end

  # read the list of whitelisted and required configs
  whitelist = File.read('config/.whitelist').split("\n")
  required  = File.read('config/.required').split("\n")

  loader = ConfigLoader.new({
    'config'    => raw_configs,
    'required'  => required,
    'whitelist' => whitelist
  })
```

```ruby
module TodoApp
end

TodoApp::CONFIG          = loader.config
TodoApp::CONFIG_RACK_APP = ConfigRackApp.new(loader.masked_config)

rescue
  msg = "Error loading configuration"
  msg << "\n  "
  msg << $!.message

  abort msg
end
```

The initializer loads two other files in the `lib` folder. The initializer also assumes that there are two newline-separated lists for required and whitelisted configurations stored in the `config` folder. Let's look at what these lists contain. The `.required` file in this case just has a single entry:

```
RE09_REDIS_URL
```

And the `.whitelist` file is similarly simple:

```
RE09_TODO_STORE
RE09_REDIS_URL
```

Notice that we use the `RE09_` prefix and a simple regular expression to find all the relevant entries in `ENV` for our app. Now let's look at `lib/config_loader.rb`, which handles validation and masking:

```ruby
class ConfigLoader
  attr_reader :config, :masked_config

  def initialize(opts={})
    if ! opts['config'].is_a?(Hash)
      raise "Expected 'config' to be a Hash, got #{opts['config'].class}"
    end

    @config    = opts['config']
    @whitelist = opts['whitelist'] || []
    @required  = opts['required']  || []

    self.class.check_required_keys!(@config, @required)
```

```
      @masked_config = self.class.mask_hash(@config, @whitelist)
    end

    class << self
      def check_required_keys!(hsh, required)
        missing_keys = required.select { |k| ! hsh.has_key?(k) }

        if ! missing_keys.empty?
          pluralized = if missing_keys.size == 1
            'key'
          else
            'keys'
          end

          raise "Missing required #{pluralized}: #{missing_keys.join(',
')}"
        else
          true
        end
      end

      def mask_hash(hsh, whitelist)
        hsh.inject({}) do |masked, (k,v)|
          masked[k] = if whitelist.include?(k)
            v
          else
            '[MASKED]'
          end

          masked
        end
      end
    end
end
```

This is straightforward but it's worth pointing out that we're separating the loading, detection, and storage of the configuration values. This is important for keeping the configuration mechanism flexible. Finally, let's look at the Rack app that reports the loaded configuration, which is defined in `lib/config_rack_app.rb`:

```
require 'json'

class ConfigRackApp
  def initialize(config)
```

```
    if ! config.is_a?(Hash)
      raise "Expected a Hash, got a #{config.class}"
    end

    @config = config
  end

  def call(env)
    json_body = JSON.pretty_generate(@config)

    [
      200,                                   # HTTP status code
      {'Content-type' => 'application/json'}, # HTTP headers
      [ json_body ]                          # HTTP body
    ]
  end
end
```

This is also pretty simple and we've seen several examples of Rack apps already in *Chapter 7, Building an App from the Outside In with Behavior-Driven Development* and *Chapter 8, Tackling the Challenges of End-to-end Testing,* so we won't spend any time explaining how it works.

We're ready to start up our app and hit the /varz.json endpoint:

```
● ● ●                            Terminal
$ ./start.sh
[2015-12-23 21:57:34] INFO  WEBrick 1.3.1
[2015-12-23 21:57:34] INFO  ruby 2.2.3 (2015-08-18) [x86_64-darwin14]
[2015-12-23 21:57:34] INFO  WEBrick::HTTPServer#start: pid=16368 port=9292
```

We can see that the expected configurations are reported and the whitelist is applied correctly to the two values defined in the .whitelist file:

```
● ● ●                            Terminal
$ curl http://localhost:9292/varz.json
{

  "RE09_REDIS_URL": "redis://127.0.0.1:6379/0",
  "RE09_TODO_STORE": "REDIS",
  "RE09_REDIS_PASSWORD": "[MASKED]"
}
$
```

You should experiment with modifying the `.env`, `.required`, and `.whitelist` files to make sure everything works as expected and you understand how all this fits together. We'll end by starting the app with some overrides and see what happens:

```
● ● ●                          Terminal
$ RE09_FOO=BAR RE09_REDIS_URL=some_url ./start.sh
skipping RE09_REDIS_URL in file (already set to 'some_url')
[2015-12-23 22:04:10] INFO  WEBrick 1.3.1
[2015-12-23 22:04:10] INFO  ruby 2.2.3 (2015-08-18) [x86_64-darwin14]
[2015-12-23 22:04:10] INFO  WEBrick::HTTPServer#start: pid=17522 port=9292
```

It works! The extra config `RE09_FOO` is reported and masked. The override value for `RE09_REDIS_URL` is also properly set:

```
● ● ●                          Terminal
$ curl http://localhost:9292/varz.json
{
    "RE09_REDIS_URL": "some_url",
    "RE09_TODO_STORE": "REDIS",
    "RE09_REDIS_PASSWORD": "[MASKED]",
    "RE09_FOO": "[MASKED]"
}
$
```

Let's conclude with some important details regarding the `.env` file.

This should never be checked into version control. The whole point of configuration management is to separate configuration from our app code. We can add a placeholder file called `.env.example` with reasonable suggested values for local development and check that into version control instead.

This leads to another issue: where is the `.env` file supposed to come from? This is entirely up to you. You can store it in a private repository and retrieve it whenever it is needed. You can use a sophisticated configuration management tool such as `etcd` or `consul` and then generate the `.env` file. You can also bypass the file altogether and use another means of reading the configuration values and loading them into the environment by modifying the `env-echo.sh` script to, for example, read the configurations from a database.

Given the modular design of the configuration management code we've developed, the rest should just work without any change.

For testing purposes, you can create a dedicated config file, `.env.test`, and load that instead of `.env` when running tests.

Summary

In this chapter, we learned about the concept of configurability and its relation to testability. We configured an app using environment variables and some simple Unix tools. We then enhanced the example to address real-world concerns, such as validation of config files, namespacing of configurations, and safe reporting of loaded values.

10
Odds and Ends

In this chapter, we will finish our journey through RSpec by learning about a few miscellaneous topics which are important but which didn't quite fit into the flow of the preceding chapters, which focused on a smooth progression through RSpec's essential features.

Here is what we will cover in this chapter:

- Reducing duplication with shared example groups
- Mocking time
- Detecting false negatives and false positives
- Testing mixins with dummy containers

Reducing duplication with shared example groups

Often, similar assertions are made in multiple tests, which leads to duplication of code. One of the ways this can be addressed is with RSpec's shared example groups, which allow you to reuse a set of tests to fit different situations.

Let's say we have a few tests that repeat the same assertion:

```
describe AddressValidator
  it "valid? returns false for incomplete address" do
    expect(AddressValidator.valid?(address)).to eq(false)
  end
  context "address contains invalid characters" do
    let(:address) { "$123% Any^ St., Anytown, CA, USA 12345" }
    it "valid? returns false for incomplete address" do
      expect(AddressValidator.valid?(address)).to eq(false)
```

```
      end
    end
    context "address is a String" do
      let(:address) { "123 Any St., Anytown" }
      it "valid? returns false for incomplete address" do
        expect(AddressValidator.valid?(address)).to eq(false)
      end
    end
  end
```

We can see that we keep repeating the same assertion in each test:

```
expect(AddressValidator.valid?(address)).to eq(false)
```

As a first step, let's create a shared example group to deal with invalid addresses:

```
shared_examples_for "invalid address" do
  it "valid? returns false" do
    expect(AddressValidator.valid?(address)).to eq(false)
  end
end
```

The shared examples are defined using `shared_examples_for` and executed with `it_behaves_like`. To execute the shared example above, we would use the following code:

```
# assume address is defined in this context (e.g. with let)
it_behaves_like "invalid address"
```

When defining a shared example group, the first argument is a name, which is used when executing the shared example group. It is important to think of a good name that will be meaningful when used with `it_behaves_like`.

In the example above, we pass values to the shared example group using `let`. Notice that we do not define `address` within the shared example group, so an error would be raised if `address` is not defined within the context where we called `it_behaves_like`.

There is another way of setting context for a shared example group with a block argument passed to `it_behaves_like`:

```
it_behaves_like "invalid address" do
  let(:address) { street: "123 Any Street", city: "Anytown" }
end
```

A complete spec using shared examples would look like the following:

```
describe AddressValidator do
```

```
shared_examples_for "invalid address" do
  it "valid? returns false" do
    expect(AddressValidator.valid?(address)).to eq(false)
  end
end
shared_examples_for "valid address" do
  it "valid? returns true" do
    expect(AddressValidator.valid?(address)).to eq(true)
  end
end
let(:address) { { street: street, city: city } }
let(:street)  { "123 Any Street"                }
let(:city)    { "Anytown"                       }
it_behaves_like "invalid address"
it_behaves_like "invalid address" do
  let(:address) { "123 Any St., Anytown" }
end

it_behaves_like "valid address" do
  let(:address) { "123 Any St., Anytown, CA, USA, 12345" }
end
it_behaves_like "valid address" do
  let(:address) do
    {
      street:       "123 Any Street",
      city:         "Anytown",
      region:       "Anyplace",
      country:      "Anyland",
      postal_code:  "123456"
    }
  end
end
end
```

There is another way of passing values to a shared example group without relying on the context where the group is called. We specify a block variable in the definition of the shared example group. This allows values to be passed to it_behaves_like as additional arguments after the name:

```
shared_examples_for "invalid address" do |addr|
  it "valid? returns false" do
    expect(AddressValidator.valid?(addr)).to eq(false)
  end
end
it_behaves_like "invalid address", "123 Any St., Anytown"
```

Following this style, our spec now looks like the following:

```
describe AddressValidator do
  shared_examples_for "invalid address" do |addr|
    it "valid? returns false" do
      expect(AddressValidator.valid?(addr)).to eq(false)
    end
  end
  shared_examples_for "valid address" do |addr|
    it "valid? returns true" do
      expect(AddressValidator.valid?(addr)).to eq(true)
    end
  end
  it_behaves_like("invalid address", {
    street: "123 Any Street",
    city:   "Anytown"
  })
  it_behaves_like "invalid address", "123 Any St., Anytown"
  it_behaves_like(
    "invalid address",
    "$123% Any^ St., Anytown, CA, USA, 12345"
  )

  it_behaves_like(
    "valid address",
    "123 Any St., Anytown, CA, USA, 12345"
  )
  it_behaves_like("valid address",  {
    street:       "123 Any Street",
    city:         "Anytown",
    region:       "Anyplace",
    country:      "Anyland",
    postal_code:  "123456"
  })
end
```

Deciding which approach to use to pass variables depends on the situation, as well as your own style. Using the context (for example, values defined by `let`) introduces more complexity but gives you more power. This is useful but can introduce bugs and make your test code more difficult to understand. Passing in extra variables to `it_behaves_like` is simple, but you can wind up with a lot of duplication. You can even combine the two, although I would advise against it.

There is no limit to how many `describe`, `context`, and `it` blocks that a shared example group can have. You can also nest shared example groups within a shared example group. This is a very powerful feature, but it usually leads to very complex test code, which is not reliable or easy to maintain. However, there are some good use cases, especially when you have multiple objects that do the same thing.

Let's say we were refactoring our `AddressValidator` to use an external service provided by a government postal service. We could see if the new validator behaved like the old one by using shared example groups to encapsulate the entire spec for `AddressValidator`:

```
shared_examples_for "address validation module" do
  shared_examples_for "invalid address" do |addr|
    it "valid? returns false" do
      expect(validator.valid?(addr)).to eq(false)
    end
  end
  shared_examples_for "valid address" do |addr|
    it "valid? returns true" do
      expect(validator.valid?(addr)).to eq(true)
    end
  end
  it_behaves_like("invalid address", {
    street: "123 Any Street",
    city:   "Anytown"
  })
  it_behaves_like "invalid address", "123 Any St., Anytown"
  it_behaves_like(
    "invalid address",
    "$123% Any^ St., Anytown, CA, USA, 12345"
  )

  it_behaves_like(
    "valid address",
    "123 Any St., Anytown, CA, USA, 12345"
  )
  it_behaves_like("valid address",  {
    street:       "123 Any Street",
    city:         "Anytown",
    region:       "Anyplace",
    country:      "Anyland",
    postal_code:  "123456"
  })
end
```

Now we can create separate tests for `AddressValidator` and `NewAddressValidator`:

```
describe AddressValidator do
  subject(:validator) { AddressValidator }
  it_behaves_like "address validation module"
end

describe NewAddressValidator do
  subject(:validator) { NewAddressValidator }
  it_behaves_like "address validation module"

  # add specs for new features here
end
```

Let's look at another example where we can use shared example groups. Let's go back to the tests we wrote for errors in `WeatherQuery` back in *Chapter 2, Specifying Behavior with Examples and Matchers*. We can reduce duplication here and make it easier to test for more types of errors by using shared example groups. Here's what we had in *Chapter 2, Specifying Behavior with Examples and Matchers*:

```
describe WeatherQuery do
  describe '.forecast' do
   context 'network errors' do
      let(:custom_error) { WeatherQuery::NetworkError }

      before do
        expect(Net::HTTP).to receive(:get)
                              .and_raise(err_to_raise)
      end

      context 'timeouts' do
        let(:err_to_raise) { Timeout::Error }

        it 'handles the error' do
          expect{
            WeatherQuery.forecast("Antarctica")
          }.to raise_error(custom_error, "Request timed out")
        end
      end

      context 'invalud URI' do
        let(:err_to_raise) { URI::InvalidURIError }

        it 'handles the error' do
```

```
        expect{
          WeatherQuery.forecast("Antarctica")
        }.to raise_error(custom_error, "Bad place name: Antarctica")
      end
    end

    context 'socket errors' do
      let(:err_to_raise) { SocketError }

      it 'handles the error' do
        expect{
          WeatherQuery.forecast("Antarctica")
        }.to raise_error(custom_error, /Could not reach http:\/\//)
      end
    end
  end

  let(:xml_response) do
    %q(
      <?xml version="1.0" encoding="utf-8"?>
      <current>
        <weather number="800" value="Sky is Clear" icon="01n"/>
      </current>
    )
  end

  it "raises a NetworkError if response is not JSON" do
    expect(WeatherQuery).to receive(:http)
      .with('Antarctica')
      .and_return(xml_response)

    expect{
      WeatherQuery.forecast("Antarctica")
    }.to raise_error(
      WeatherQuery::NetworkError, "Bad response"
    )
  end
  end
end
```

Now let's create a shared example group for "network errors" that we can reuse. Here's what that would look like:

```
describe WeatherQuery do
  describe '.forecast' do
```

```
shared_examples_for "network errors" do |err_to_raise, msg|
  before do
    expect(Net::HTTP).to receive(:get)
                            .and_raise(err_to_raise)
  end

  let(:expected_error)   { WeatherQuery::NetworkError }

  it "raises a NetworkError instead of #{err_to_raise}" do
    expect{
      WeatherQuery.forecast("Antarctica")
    }.to raise_error(expected_error, msg)
  end
end

it_behaves_like "network errors",
  Timeout::Error,
  "Request timed out"

it_behaves_like "network errors",
  URI::InvalidURIError
  "Bad place name: Antarctica"

it_behaves_like "network errors",
  SocketError,
  /Could not reach http:\/\//

let(:xml_response) do
  %q(
    <?xml version="1.0" encoding="utf-8"?>
    <current>
      <weather number="800" value="Sky is Clear" icon="01n"/>
    </current>
  )
end

it "raises a NetworkError if response is not JSON" do
  expect(WeatherQuery).to receive(:http)
    .with('Antarctica')
    .and_return(xml_response)

  expect{
    WeatherQuery.forecast("Antarctica")
  }.to raise_error(
```

```
          WeatherQuery::NetworkError, "Bad response"
        )
      end
    end
  end
```

As we can see, this is shorter and easier to read.

Mocking time

Code that deals with time and dates can be very difficult to test. Code can behave differently based on the time of day or the day of the year. Time is a peculiar type of state which we can usually ignore in our code, but when code interacts directly with time, we have to face the complexities of time. Time-related bugs can be especially tricky, dangerous, and difficult to reproduce. Time is also related intrinsically to place, since we have to take time zones into account, as well as daylight saving time, which varies from country to country (and from region to region within certain countries).

Fortunately, there are libraries specifically designed to mock time. In this section, we'll learn how to use the Timecop gem (https://github.com/travisjeffery/timecop) to test time-related code.

Let's work with a Schedule class that allows appointments to be created. We don't want appointments to be made for any date in the past. We can test for this without any special code, as follows:

```
describe Schedule do
  subject(:schedule) { Schedule.new }

  describe '.add' do
    it "does not allow appointments for past dates" do
      expect{
        schedule.add(Time.now - 1 , "Ruby meetup")
      }.to raise_error("Can't add a date in the past")
    end
  end
end
```

Another simple rule we would like is to require two business days' notice for an appointment. That is, there have to be two working days between the current time and the desired appointment time. Now things get more difficult, as we have to know which days are business days in order to write a test. We can't pick a date in the past, since our code doesn't allow that. We could try to pick a date in the future, but then as soon as that date passed, our tests would begin to fail, since we'd be trying to add a past date. We could pick a date far out in the future, say 200 years from now, to try to avoid the problem, but then we would have a very weird test, which would work only because it was testing for totally unrealistic inputs.

Furthermore, there are many common bugs that come up when dealing with days at the end of the week, end of the month, or right before a holiday. Testing that our scheduling code works correctly on such dates would be very useful.

Finally, the definition of a business day varies from region to region. If our code was used in different locales, we would have to ensure that we had properly taken local holiday schedules and time zones into account.

To address all of these issues, we can mock out time using `Timecop`. Although we could try to mock time ourselves by changing the behavior of `Time.now`, this is difficult and dangerous. Time is handled by three different classes in Ruby (`Time`, `Date`, and `DateTime`), so we have to mock multiple methods and ensure that we unmock all of them after our tests. Changing time can also have all kinds of unintended side effects since so many libraries depend on time in one way or another. Therefore, using a dedicated, robust library like `Timecop` is a better alternative.

`Timecop` gives us a few methods to mock time. We'll start with `Timecop.travel`, which allows us to change the current time to any time in the past or future. Let's say we want to set the current time to November 20, 2013:

```
Timecop.travel(Time.local(2013, 11, 20))
```

An important thing to note is that `Timecop` does not reset the time back to normal automatically if we use it in this simple way. It is up to us to do this manually, using the `Timecop.return` method.

This can be done with an `after` or `around` hook, but I strongly recommend that you use the block version of the `travel` method to ensure you never mock time outside the explicit cases where you need to:

```
Timecop.travel(Time.local(2013, 11, 20)) do
  ...
end
```

With this code, the time is mocked only within the block. Once we exit the block, everything is back to normal. Timecop has a safe mode that can force you to use only the block syntax. It is a very good idea to enable safe mode in your RSpec configuration (for example, `spec_helper.rb`) as follows:

```
Timecop.safe_mode = true
```

Using `Timecop`, we can write a simple test that mocks a date before a holiday:

```
require 'Timecop'

Timecop.safe_mode = true
# with Timecop
describe Schedule do
  subject(:schedule) { Schedule.new }
  let(:turkey_day) { Date.parse('November 28, 2013') }

  describe '.add' do
    it "does not allow appointments on holidays" do
      Timecop.travel(turkey_day - 5) do
        expect{
          schedule.add(turkey_day.to_time, "Eat turkey!")
        }.to raise_error(/November 28, 2013 is a holiday/)
      end
    end
  end
end
```

How does this work? `Timecop` monkey patches `Time.new`, `Time.now`, `Date.today`, and `DateTime.now` to set them to the mocked time. `Timecop` also allows you to freeze time so that the system timer does not move at all by using `Timecop.freeze`. This can be useful for cases where small changes in time will affect your test results. Finally, `Timecop` also allows you to speed up the passage of time using `Timecop.scale`, which can be helpful if you are testing code that runs in long intervals, such as once a day or once a month.

Detecting false negatives and false positives

Tests can fool us with failures when the code actually works fine (false negatives) and successes when the code is broken (false positives). There is no way to completely eliminate false results, but we can reduce their likelihood by keeping tests simple and doing sanity checks. Sometimes our tests might seem like they are not doing enough, or we may seem to be checking for redundant things that we expect never to break. That is simply the price we have to pay to minimize the chance that our tests are fooling us.

Let's cover three useful tactics to reduce false results:

- Sanity checks
- Tests for the opposite case
- Increased specificity of assertions

Detecting false results is a fundamental concern of testing, so the tests all throughout this chapter (and the rest of the book) include measures to reduce false results. For example, let's go back to three `before` hooks in three different tests that we defined in *Chapter 3, Taking Control of State with Doubles and Hooks*, each of which includes a sanity check:

```
before do
  expect(WeatherQuery).to receive(:http).
                          once.
                          and_return(json_response)

  actual = WeatherQuery.send(:cache)
  expect(actual).to eq({})
end

before do
  expect(WeatherQuery.history).to eq([])
  allow(WeatherQuery).to receive(:http).and_return("{}")
end

before do
  expect(WeatherQuery.api_request_count).to eq(0)
  allow(WeatherQuery).to receive(:http).and_return("{}")
end
```

Notice that each hook includes an assertion about a default state for `cache` (empty `Hash`), `history` (empty `Array`), and `api_request_count` (zero (`0`)). The purpose of these is not to test that we have a good default value in our code, but to catch unexpected leakage between tests. If, for some reason, our test started with a non-empty `cache` or `history` or a non-zero `api_request_count`, we could get all kinds of strange behavior, since we probably have not properly cleared our state from a previous test. If that behavior caused a test to pass that should have failed, we would not have any reason to examine the situation further. However, with these sanity checks in our `before` hooks, any anomalies related to state will immediately trigger a failure even before our test case is run.

The next tactic we'll cover is to test for the opposite case. Basically, we want to take a passing test and force it to fail in order to convince ourselves that things work the way we expect them to. Let's say we have a configuration management class called `Configurator` which reads a YAML file that defines a `Hash`. In case the YAML file is not there, we don't want to raise an error. We just want to return an empty `Hash` for our configuration. Our test code may look like this:

```
describe Configurator do
  context 'YAML file not present' do
    it "returns an empty hash" do
      actual = Configurator.load('this_is_not_a_file.yml')
      expect(actual).to eq({})
    end
  end
end
```

Now let's say we have an implementation for our `Configurator` that looks for a JSON file rather than a YAML file:

```
require 'json'

class Configurator
  def self.load(path)
    if File.exists?(path)
      JSON.parse(File.read(path))
    else
      {}
    end
  end
end
```

When we run our test, it will pass, because our file does not exist. As soon as we try to use our code with a real YAML file, however, we will get a JSON::ParserError (unless the YAML in the file actually contains JSON, which is, in fact, a valid subset of YAML). So here we have a false positive. To test the opposite case, we simply need to add a test for the case when the file is present. Alternatively we can do a quick check without adding any new test code by creating a YAML file and running the test again. A new test case would look like this:

```
context 'YAML file present' do
  let(:path) { 'this_is_not_a_file.yml' }
  it "returns an empty hash" do
    expect(File).to receive(:exists?).
                    with(path).
                    and_return(true)
    expect(File).to receive(:read).
                    with(path).
                    and_return("")
    actual = Configurator.load(path)
    expect(actual).to eq({})
  end
end
```

Here we've mocked the filesystem calls. When we run our tests, we will now get a JSON::ParserError exception, which alerts us to the silly mistake we have in our code. Mistakes like these seem silly in hindsight, but they happen all the time. If you think about how much damage can be done by a mistake in a single line of code, and about how many thousands, or even millions, of lines of code are executed in today's software, you'll begin to appreciate the value of testing for false results.

Now let's say we want to raise an error if the YAML file is not found. Our code would now be as follows:

```
require 'yaml'
class Configurator
  def self.load(path)
    if File.exists?(path)
      YAML.load_file(path)
    else
      raise "Couldn't find file : #{path}"
    end
  end
end
```

We might dash off a quick test such as the following:

```
describe Configurator do
  context 'YAML file not present' do
    it "raises an error" do
      expect{
        Configurator.load
      }.to raise_error
    end
  end
end
```

This test would pass just fine. In fact, it is a false positive, because the error being raised is an `ArgumentError` because we've forgotten to pass the path to the `Configurator.load` method! To confirm this, we can comment out the `raise` line in `Configurator.load` and re-run the test, which will still pass even though we aren't raising any errors on purpose.

To address this issue, we need to increase the specificity of our assertion. The simplest way to do this is to check that the error message is one that we expect:

```
describe Configurator do
  context 'YAML file not present' do
    it "raises an error" do
      expect{
        Configurator.load
      }.to raise_error(/Couldn't find file/)
    end
  end
end
```

Running our test this time will result in a failure:

```
Failure/Error: expect{
  expected Exception with message matching /Couldn't find file/, got
  #<ArgumentError: wrong number of arguments (0 for 1)>
```

This lets us know that there is something unexpected going on with our test. We could also test for the error class. This is useful when dealing with multiple kinds of error.

Testing mixins with dummy containers

Ruby's mixin functionality can be very useful. Modules can group together useful features that can be added at runtime to any class. However, given the dynamic nature of Ruby, testing the mixin features of a module can be tricky.

Let's go back to the AddressValidator module we worked with in previous sections of this chapter and in *Chapter 1, Exploring Testability from Unit Tests to Behavior-Driven Development* and *Chapter 2, Specifying Behavior with Examples and Matchers*. We want to make this module into a mixin that we can add to any object with an address method. Then we can call address_valid? on the object to trigger all the validations.

Regardless of the complexity of the metaprogramming involved with a mixin, we can still treat it as a normal test case with a known input and expected output. The input, in this case, is not a set of arguments to a method, but a whole class into which we mix in the AddressValidator module:

```
describe AddressValidator do
  class Dummy
    attr_accessor :address

    include AddressValidator
  end
  subject(:addressable) { Dummy.new }

  it "should have an address_valid? method" do
    expect(addressable).to respond_to(:address_valid?)
  end
end
```

This is very simple. Just note the fact that we define a class within the describe block and then include the module we are testing. We can make more complex assertions with ease.

Now let's look at an example that involves more metaprogramming. We want to create a module that will add a cheesy version of each method defined on the class in which it is included. If the class contained an address method, then including this silly module would add an address_with_cheese method:

```
module Cheesy
  def self.included(base)
    base.class_eval do
      def method_missing(meth, *args, &block)
        if meth.to_s =~ /_with_cheese$/
          without_cheese = meth.to_s.gsub(/_with_cheese$/, '')
```

```ruby
        if respond_to?(without_cheese)
          "#{without_cheese} is better with cheese!"
        else
          "Don't know how to add cheese to #{without_cheese}!"
        end
      else
        super
      end
    end

    def respond_to?(meth, include_private = false)
      if meth.to_s =~ /_with_cheese$/
        without_cheese = meth.to_s.gsub(/_with_cheese$/, '')

        respond_to?(without_cheese)
      else
        super
      end
    end
  end
end


describe Cheesy do
  class Dummy
    include Cheesy
  end
  subject(:cheesed) { Dummy.new }

  it "has an inspect_with_cheese method" do
    expect(cheesed).to respond_to(:inspect_with_cheese)
  end

  it "adds cheese to inspect" do
    actual = cheesed.inspect_with_cheese
    expect(actual).to eq("inspect is better with cheese!")
  end

  it "doesn't add cheese to foobar" do
    actual   = cheesed.foobar_with_cheese
    expected = "Don't know how to add cheese to foobar!"
    expect(actual).to eq(expected)
  end
end
```

We've done a bit of metaprogramming here and have leveraged the fact that any Ruby `Object` has an `inspect` method. Again, the only trick here is that we've defined a throwaway `Dummy` class into which we've included our `mixin` module. In theory, we could create more complex dummy classes to test various scenarios. That can be tricky and lead to unreliable and unmaintainable code. In general, mixins should avoid complex interactions with the classes that they extend.

Summary

In this chapter, we covered a handful of *odds and ends* related to reducing duplication, mocking time, detecting false results, and testing mixins.

Index

A

AngularJS
  home page link 130
application code
  improving 31-34
automated tests 2

B

behavior-driven development (BDD)
  about 15, 109
  cons 160
  exploring 110, 111
  pros 160
  running 119, 120
black-box JavaScript tests
  using, with real browser 107, 108
built-in matchers
  about 23
  reference link 23
Bundler
  about 176
  reference link 119

C

Capybara
  about 99
  features 102
  integrating, with RSpec 103-105
  need for 106, 107
  starting with 100-103

configuration
  about 168
  examples 168
  importance 168
configuration manager 173-183
context
  using 20-23
continuous integration (CI) 70
Cucumber example 15
custom helpers
  used, for mocking HTTP responses 86, 87
custom matchers 24-26

D

double 45
dummy containers
  used, for testing mixins 200-202
duplication
  reducing, with shared example
      groups 185-191

E

end-to end testing, challenges
  API, defining 133-155
  view, building 127-133
  view, finishing 157-160
errors
  reference link 38
  testing for 35-40
executable documentation 15
external services
  importance 85, 86

86765741R00122